Let Us Start with Light

An Enquiry into Reality, Time, and the Illusion of Self

Vivek Sharma

Let Us Start with Light

An Enquiry into Reality, Time, and the Illusion of Self

First published 2026 | Melbourne, Australia
Publisher: Stillpoint Books

ISBN: 978–1–7646128–9–0

DEDICATION

To the masters, scientists, mystics, and silent witnesses – in whom the search for truth arose, and dissolved.

CONTENTS

ACKNOWLEDGMENTS

This book would not exist without a chance encounter that took place many years ago with a hidden mystic. The mystic asked nothing of those who came into his presence except that they look inward – directly, honestly, and beyond the comfort of thought–based perceptions and ego. Whatever clarity finds expression in these pages traces back to that invitation, though the words themselves are entirely my own responsibility.

The debt is one that cannot be repaid, only carried forward.

PREFACE

There comes a point – not always dramatic, not always visible – when something subtle begins to loosen.

Not in the world, but in the way the world is held.

What once seemed certain begins to feel less solid.
What once appeared obvious starts to invite questions.

And quietly, almost imperceptibly, the centre from which we experience life begins to shift.

This book was not written to provide answers.

It was not written to defend a philosophy or ideology, promote a belief, or offer a system to follow.

If anything, it moves in the opposite direction.

It begins with what appears to be the most reliable ground we have – the physical world.

Light.
Matter.
Time.
Space.

The very things we trust – to tell us what is real.

But as we look more closely – through science, through observation, through careful attention and insights – that awareness begins to behave in unexpected ways.

What appears solid reveals itself as mostly empty.
What seems continuous is discovered to be discontinuous.
What feels immediate is already in the past.

From there, the enquiry turns inward.

Perception.
Thought.
Memory.
The sense of being someone – a centre, an "I", or a "me".

We assume this centre exists – the "person" we think we are.

We rarely question it.

And yet, when examined closely, it becomes increasingly difficult to locate.

Across cultures, across centuries, there have been those who investigated this directly.

Not as belief.
Not as theory.
But as lived enquiry.

Some spoke of no–self.
Some of emptiness.
Some of pure awareness.
Some of unity.

Their words differ.

But there is a quiet convergence in what they point to.

At the same time, modern science has taken its own path – probing matter, particles, natural forces, energy, space, and the brain.

It has mapped complexity with extraordinary precision.

And yet, when it comes to the nature of experience itself – to consciousness – it stands at a threshold.

Describing, but not fully explaining.
This book moves between these two currents.

In doing so, the language of this book occasionally draws from fields such as quantum physics, neuroscience, and contemplative traditions.

These are not used as frameworks to explain reality in a final sense, nor as authorities to be believed.

Quantum physics, at its edges, reveals a world that does not behave in ways our intuition expects – where certainty gives way to probability, and observation appears inseparable from what is observed.

Neuroscience explores the brain with remarkable precision, yet the simple fact of experience – of being aware – remains deeply elusive.

Spiritual traditions, in their most direct expressions, do not offer explanations, but invitations – to look, to question, and to see for oneself.

Not to merge them artificially.
Not to prove one through the other.

But to allow a space where both can be seen clearly –
and where their implications can unfold.

What follows is not a journey in the conventional sense.

Because a journey assumes distance.
A starting point.
A destination.
A traveller moving between them.

Here, even that assumption is gently questioned.

You are not asked to believe anything.
You are not asked to accept or reject.
Only to look.

And perhaps, somewhere along the way,

to notice something simple–

That is what you have been seeking may not be elsewhere.
And may not belong to anyone.

If this book does anything at all, let it not give you conclusions.
Let it take away what never quite held.
A note on how this book moves.

The first two parts move through the language of science and philosophy. They are largely expository, drawing on physics, neuroscience, and the history of ideas. The third part turns toward consciousness directly – examining what thinkers and traditions have said about awareness, the soul, and the nature of the self.

The fourth part is different again: quieter, more personal, closer to the texture of immediate experience. The register shifts as the enquiry deepens. This is intentional. Each part asks something different of the reader, in the same way that a conversation might begin with questions about the world and end with something harder to name.

So, we begin.

With light.

PART I: THE ILLUSION OF SOLIDITY

ALL THAT ILLUMINATES

Let's talk about light.

Why light?

Because light gives us the measure of the world we inhabit and the universe we see around us. Through light we perceive travel, distance, space, reflection, colours, illumination – and, perhaps most importantly, *Time.*

Time, as we understand it and perceive it, unfolds through light. It allows events to appear ordered and structured, separated, measurable. From this emerges the sense of history – past, present, and future – a seemingly linear thread stretching from the birth of the universe to this very moment.

Through this thread we tell the story of existence: from the early formation of stars and planets to human evolution - the unfolding theories of Darwinian evolution; from ancient civilisations and early mythologies to mysticism, empires, wars, revolutions, and the rise of religions; from sages and philosophers to cultures, traditions, music, art and the constant development of human experience.

In our own era, that same unfolding appears in scientific discovery, space exploration, technological revolutions – and, again, we see advancement of human life, new conflicts, and new questions. Amidst all the sparkles of life, a deep unease remains – about uncertainties, about the purpose, meaning, and value of life. Most prominently, what exists after life.

Seen this way, existence appears to move in a continuous current –

always advancing, always evolving – as though reality itself were engaged in a perpetual journey forward.

Or so we are told.
So, we perceive.

In 1905, Einstein created an enigma for us. He established that nothing travels faster than light in this universe. According to his theory of Special Relativity, nothing with mass can travel at or above the speed of light. The speed of light in vacuum – approximately 299,792 kilometres per second – is the cosmic speed limit. As an object with mass moves faster and faster toward the speed of light, it requires more and more energy to keep accelerating. Eventually the energy needed becomes infinite, which means no physical object can ever reach the speed of light.

Light, therefore, is not merely an illumination. It is the ruler by which the universe becomes measurable. Every distance we calculate, every motion we detect, and every moment we record is ultimately determined by how light travels through space. In this sense, the observable universe is revealed to us through light. Without it, there would be no scale of distance, no chronology of events, no story of cosmic history unfolding across billions of years.

Yet, hidden within this very measure lies a paradox.

In a quiet corner of the cosmos, on top of a stoney hill, lived an old woman known as the Weaver. She did not weave wool or silk. She spent her days catching light in silver jars and polishing glass until it was as clear as empty space.

One evening, a student came to her, his heart heavy with the weight of years.

"Everything I love is disappearing," the student confessed. "My childhood home is a ruin, my mentors are all long gone, and the songs and moments of my youth have faded into the wind. Time is a thief that leaves no trace of what it steals."

The Weaver did not offer words of comfort. Instead, she led him to the centre of the plateau, where a telescope of impossible proportions stood aimed at the blackest part of the sky.

"Twenty light–years from here," the Weaver said, pointing a gnarled finger toward a faint, silver pinhole in the distance, "floats a mirror of ancient glass. It is so far that your eyes see it only as a cold spark. But this telescope, it is a bridge across the silence. It gathers

the scattered whispers of the past."

The student pressed his eye to the lens. At first, there was only darkness. Then, like a ghost materialising from a fog, a scene appeared–sharp, vibrant, and drenched in a sun he hadn't felt in decades.

He gasped. He didn't see the dark plateau or the Weaver. He saw a sun–lit kitchen from his youth. He saw a woman – his mother – pouring tea into a blue ceramic cup. She looked toward the window, smiling at something she saw outside in the garden.

"That cup broke a lifetime ago," the student whispered, his breath fogging the eyepiece. "And my mother. She has been gone for five years. How am I seeing her now?"

"You are seeing the 'Then' in the 'Now'," the Weaver replied softly. "The light that touched her face forty years ago travelled twenty years through the dark to reach that mirror. It bounced, and it has spent the last twenty years racing back to this very spot. You are catching the ghosts of four decades ago."

The student reached out, his fingers trembling as if he could reach through the glass and touch the steam rising from the tea. "If I watch long enough," he asked, "will she turn toward me? Will she see me standing here?"

The Weaver sighed, a sound like shifting sand. "She will turn, but she is not turning toward you. She is turning towards the boy you were forty years ago, playing on the grass. You are a ghost watching a ghost. The telescope does not bring the past back to life; it only reveals that the past never truly stopped happening. It is simply a matter of where you stand and how much light you can catch."

The student stayed at the lens until the stars began to pale. He realised then that the universe was not a graveyard of lost moments, but a vast, radiating library. Every tear shed, every secret whispered, and every tea–pour was still travelling through the void, etched into the flight of photons, waiting for a lens large enough to find them again.

He stepped away from the telescope, no longer feeling like a victim of time. He understood now that he, too, was currently being broadcast to the stars–an eternal masterpiece of light, racing forever toward the edge of the world.

We think that we experience the world as a synchronised, real–time movie, but physics tells us we are actually living in a fragmented collage of different histories. The past isn't "gone"– it is just "elsewhere." In modern physics, this idea echoes a deeper principle: information about physical events is not easily erased from the universe. Nothing you have ever seen has been "real time." We live in a sensory lag.

When you look at the Moon, you see it as it was 1.3 seconds ago.

When you look at the Sun, you see it as it was 8 minutes ago; that is how much the sunlight takes to reach us.

When you look at a friend across a dinner table, you see them as they were a few nanoseconds ago.

If the Sun were to vanish this very instant, we would continue to bask in its warmth and light for eight full minutes, living in a reality that has already ceased to exist.

The light that bounced off your first birthday cake didn't vanish; it simply expanded into a sphere that is now 20, 30, or 50 light–years wide. If you could outrun that light, you could catch it. This implies that time is a "*spatial dimension*". We think of the past as a memory in our heads, but the universe treats the past as a physical coordinate in space. As Einstein established, reality is relative to the observer. Two people in different parts of the universe, moving at different speeds, will not agree on which events happened first. To one observer, a star might have already exploded; to another, it hasn't happened yet. Neither is "wrong."

Light travels at a finite speed – about 299,792 km/s.

A lightyear is the distance light travels in one year.

So, if an object is 20 light years away, the light arriving here now left that object 20 years ago.

We are not watching a movie that is being played for everyone at once. We are each sitting in our own private theatre, watching a unique edit of the universe's history based entirely on our distance from the screen. Not just that. We only see what our senses allow us to see, which is only a small fragment of cosmic reality.

One of the most moving expressions of this idea came not from a scientific paper, but from a personal letter.

In March 1955, shortly before his death, Albert Einstein wrote to the family of his lifelong friend Michele Besso:

"Now he has departed from this strange world a little ahead of me. That means nothing. People like us, who believe in physics, know that the distinction between past,

present and future is only a stubbornly persistent illusion".

This was no casual remark. It was the distilled essence of a lifetime spent rethinking the structure of reality. He emphasised that for those who understand relativity, the separation between past, present, and future is not as solid as it appears. The events of a life do not simply vanish into nothingness once the present moment moves on. They remain woven into the structure of spacetime itself.

From that perspective, Einstein suggested, Besso had not truly "gone" anywhere. His life – the conversations they shared, the moments they lived through – remained part of the universe, just located in a different region of spacetime than the moment they as now inhabiting.

To our everyday perception, time feels like a river carrying everything away. Moments appear, pass, and disappear forever.

But relativity offers a different picture. The universe may be less like a flowing river and more like an immense landscape. What we call "the present" is simply the narrow path our awareness walks through that landscape. In Einstein's universe, time did not "flow" from past to future; all moments coexisted in what physicists call the block universe. Yet, for all his insight into the illusory nature of time, Einstein's vision of reality still lacked one essential ingredient – the observer. One question remained unresolved: whose "present" is this narrow path? A universe described entirely in terms of spacetime geometry can map events with extraordinary precision, but it says little about the fact that those events are also *experienced.* The structure is there - but so is the one to whom it appears.

Science often assumes that reality and its laws exist independently of us, and that our task is simply to discover and understand them. But this leaves open a profound question: what if experience is not merely a spectator of reality, but one of its ingredients? Had Einstein brought that possibility fully into view, he may perhaps have drawn a different conclusion around the nature of the world and reality.

But in quantum physics, the observer does not remain outside the picture. At the quantum scale, reality no longer behaved in ways that classical thinking could comfortably explain. Study of quantum mechanics suggested that the act of measurement could not always be cleanly separated from the behaviour of what was measured. Einstein believed that reality existed independently of whether anyone looked at it. The moon, he famously asked, *does not cease to exist when no one is watching.* Bohr disagreed. At the quantum level, he suggested, the act of observation could *no longer be separated from what was observed.* The universe was not merely a landscape through which awareness moved; somehow, awareness itself had entered the equation. This did not mean that the world depended on us in any simple or personal way. It meant, rather, that the old picture of a fully self-contained reality, entirely untouched by observation, had begun to fracture. The universe could still be real - yet not wholly separate from the conditions under which it appeared.

Seen from this point of view, the past is not erased. It is simply no longer where we are standing.

Light and time are deeply intertwined in a way that is easy to overlook. Everything we see reaches us through light, and light does not arrive instantaneously. This means that every observation we make is, in fact, a glimpse into the past. Time creates a perception of distance, of time spent, of time to come.

Distant galaxies reveal light that began their journey millions or even billions of years before reaching our eyes. In this sense, the universe we observe is not a single moment unfolding before us, but a layered mosaic of different times arriving together through light. Yet our minds stitch these delayed signals into a seamless experience of the present. From this stitching emerges our familiar sense of past, present, and future – a continuous narrative of events progressing forward. What appears to us as the "now" of the universe is therefore not a universal moment at all, but a constructed experience shaped by the travel time of light and the way the brain organises incoming information.

Long before modern physics began questioning the nature of time, many spiritual traditions hinted at a similar mystery. In the Upanishads, the Self is described as unborn and undying – something that exists beyond the flow of temporal change. In the Bhagavad Gita, Krishna speaks of reality as that which never truly comes into being nor ceases to exist. The Sufi mystic Ibn Arabi described time as a relation perceived by the mind, not an independent reality.

Christian philosopher and master St. Augustine observed that the past survives only as memory and the future only as expectation in the mind. Buddhist teachings repeatedly emphasise that our experience unfolds only in the immediacy of the present moment. Though expressed in very different languages, these traditions share a subtle insight: the linear story of past, present, and future may not be as fundamental to reality as it appears.

Zen master Dōgen wrote:

"Time itself is being, and all being is time."

This is astonishingly close to the block–universe intuition of relativity – existence is not separate from time but woven into it. In this view, the universe is not something that unfolds moment by moment; rather, past, present, and future all coexist within a single, timeless whole, while consciousness moves through it and experiences that movement as the passage of time. From the earliest Upanishadic reflections (800 BCE) to Einstein's theory of relativity (1905 CE) lies a span of roughly 2,700 years. Across this vast period, thinkers from very different traditions questioned whether time flows in the way human intuition suggests.

Modern physics approached the question through mathematics and observation and is still trying to find all the answers. Ancient traditions approached it through philosophical enquiry and contemplative insight. Yet the light is not the only phenomenon associated with this extraordinary speed. Other processes in the universe also propagate at the speed of light, and there may be more that we are yet to fully understand. We will return to some of these later.

In modern physics, this speed represents something even deeper: it is the ultimate rate at which information and cause–and–effect can propagate through the universe. Nothing can influence anything else faster than light. A cause must always lie within the light–cone of its effect; otherwise, events could occur before the things that produced them. If information could travel instantaneously, the distinction between past and future would begin to break down, and the universe would lose the orderly sequence by which one event gives rise to another.

Before going further, it is worth pausing to ask a deceptively simple question: *what exactly is light?*

For centuries, scientists debated this question without reaching agreement. In the seventeenth century, Isaac Newton proposed that light consisted of tiny particles emitted by luminous objects. Around the same time, Christiaan Huygens argued that light behaved instead as a wave propagating through space, much like ripples moving across water.

For a long time, the wave description seemed to win the argument. Experiments with interference and diffraction clearly showed that light spreads and overlaps in ways characteristic of waves. By the nineteenth century, James Clerk Maxwell unified electricity and magnetism and demonstrated that light is an electromagnetic wave – oscillating electric and magnetic fields travelling through space.

Yet the story did not end there.

At the beginning of the twentieth century, physicists noticed something strange. When light was shone onto certain metals, electrons were sometimes knocked free from their surface. Yet this happened only when the light was above a particular frequency, no matter how bright it was. It was as though light did not arrive as a smooth, continuous wave, but in tiny packets of energy. This phenomenon became known as the Photoelectric Effect. To explain this phenomenon, Albert Einstein proposed that light is emitted and absorbed in individual quanta – later called photons. In some situations, light behaved unmistakably like a stream of particles.

Einstein later received the Nobel Prize in 1921 for his discovery. In 1926, Gilbert N. Lewis suggested the term photon in a paper published in the journal Nature. He proposed it as the name for a fundamental unit of radiant energy. Interestingly, Lewis had a somewhat different interpretation of what photons were, but the name itself was adopted by physicists and gradually became the standard term.

Physics had arrived at a strange conclusion. Light behaved like a wave in some experiments and like a particle in others.

Modern quantum theory resolved the paradox in an unexpected way: light is neither a classical wave nor a classical particle. Instead, it is a quantum entity that can exhibit properties of both depending on how it is observed.

In quantum electrodynamics, light is understood as an excitation of the electromagnetic field – a disturbance propagating through a field that fills all of space. The photon is simply the smallest measurable unit of that disturbance.

Even this description may not be the final word. Some physicists describe light not as an object travelling through space, but as a manifestation of deeper fields and interactions underlying reality itself.

What appears to us as a beam of light may therefore be less like a stream of tiny bullets and more like a ripple moving through the fundamental fabric of the universe – much like a Mexican wave in a football stadium, where the movement travels, though the people themselves remain where they are.

At this point, the nature of light becomes even more mysterious.

Light is not merely something out there in the universe. It is the means by which the universe appears to us at all. Every colour, every form, every distance, every visible thing is given through it. If this seemingly simple phenomenon already dissolves under close examination into paradox and uncertainty, then the world we so confidently call real may be far less immediate and self-evident than we imagine. To question light is already to begin questioning the certainty of appearance itself.

Imagine a simple experiment. This is the famous "Double–Slit" experiment – the smoking gun of quantum physics.

Here we go.

This experiment includes placing a light source at one end and a plain screen at the other end; kind of a projector and a screen set up. In between, a barrier is placed with two tiny slits placed side by side. Now, the light is turned on – a beam of light is directed toward a barrier. Now, if light were simply a stream of particles, like tiny bullets fired toward the barrier, we would expect a straightforward result – some particles would pass through the left slit, others through the right, producing two bright bands on the screen behind reflecting the slits.

But this is not what happens.

Instead, the screen displays a series of alternating bright and dark bands – an interference pattern. Like a wave. The screen is filled end to end with light with different intensities (i.e. darker, brighter in a pattern). This pattern is exactly what one would expect if instead of particles, waves were passing through the two slits, spreading out and overlapping, reinforcing each other in some places and cancelling out in others.

So far, nothing seems too strange, except that the experiment appears to confirm that light behaves like a wave.

Now comes the twist.

Suppose we reduce the beam of light so much that only a single photon is emitted at a time – one tiny packet of light travelling toward the slits.

Surely, if photons are individual particles, each one must pass through either the left slit or the right slit.

Yet when the experiment is repeated under these conditions, the same interference pattern gradually appears on the screen.

Even though the photons arrive one by one, the pattern suggests that each photon somehow behaves like a wave passing through both slits simultaneously and interfering with itself.

This is already astonishing.

But the experiment becomes even stranger.

Now, if we place a measuring device (such as a camera) near the slits to determine which slit the photon actually passes through, the interference pattern, wave pattern disappears. The screen now shows exactly what we would expect from ordinary particles: two simple bands corresponding to the two openings. Just a reflection of the slits. It was as if suddenly the light knew it was being watched and changed itself.

When the photon is not observed, it behaves like a wave exploring multiple possibilities. When we attempt to measure its path, it behaves like a particle choosing a definite route.

The natural question arises almost immediately.

How does the photon "know" that it is being observed?

And what exactly counts as an observation – a human eye, a measuring instrument, or something deeper?

Modern physics does not answer this question in a simple way. Quantum theory can describe the outcomes of the experiment with remarkable precision, but the underlying reason for this strange behaviours remains one of the deepest mysteries in science. It remains the subject of ongoing debate. And the answer is not easy; it touches the very fabric of our cosmos, our existence, and our reality.

The double slit experiment introduced a principle at the heart of quantum mechanics: superposition. A quantum system does not exist in one state or another until measured; it exists in all possible states at once.

Erwin Schrödinger illustrated this paradox with his famous thought experiment in 1935. Imagine a cat in a sealed box, with a mechanism triggered by the decay of a radioactive atom. If the atom decays, the cat is killed; if not, the cat lives. According to quantum principles, until the box is opened, the atom is both decayed and not decayed – and thus the cat is both alive and dead. This does not mean the cat is in a mystical limbo, but that the quantum system describing it exists as a probability wave encompassing multiple outcomes. Because, in the thought experiment, there is presumed to be no observer inside the sealed box, the cat remains entangled with those possibilities: alive, dead, or perhaps in some state that ordinary language cannot easily describe. Only when the box is opened does an observer enter the situation. At that moment, the wave collapses and only one definite reality is seen – a single state of the cat, alive or dead. Observation collapses this wave into one definite result. This strange coexistence of multiple possibilities within a single system became one of the central and most profound ideas in quantum physics: superposition. Imagine our experience in this universe as "observers".

Sounds scary? And who is observing the observer?

For the human mind, superposition challenges our sense of certainty. We prefer clear binaries: alive or dead, true or false, self or not–self. Quantum physics undermines these absolutes, suggesting reality itself is indeterminate until brought into relation with observation.

It does not stop here.

If superposition startled physicists, there was another discovery that baffled them even more. In 1935, Albert Einstein, Boris Podolsky, and Nathan Rosen (EPR) found that quantum objects seemed to behave in a strange and deeply unsettling way when separated. Imagine two particles created together and then sent far apart. Einstein dismissed this as "*spooky action at a distance.*" He believed hidden variables must exist, carrying information that determined outcomes in advance. Yet experiment after experiment confirmed that nature really does behave this way. This became the second great and profoundly mysterious idea at the heart of quantum physics: entanglement – an enigma that continues to puzzle physicists to this day.

In 1972, physicist John Clauser performed one of the first experiments of this kind, and in 1982 Alain Aspect refined it further. Pairs of photons were emitted in opposite directions and measured many metres apart. Yet the moment one photon was found to have a particular property, the other was instantly found to have the corresponding one, even though no signal could have travelled between them quickly enough. It was as though the two particles remained part of a single whole despite the distance between them.

When two quantum particles interact, they can become entangled, meaning their properties are linked no matter how far apart they are. Measure one particle's spin, and the other's spin is instantly determined – even if they are separated by lightyears.

But in 1964, physicist John Bell formulated Bell's theorem, showing that no hidden variable theory could reproduce all the predictions of quantum mechanics. Experiments in the 1980s by Alain Aspect confirmed that entangled particles violate Bell's inequalities. The correlations are real and instantaneous, defying classical notions of locality.

Entanglement reveals that quantum systems cannot be described independently. They are part of a holistic whole, in which separation is an illusion.

The question for our discerning minds is, "*Why should it concern us that a particle can exist in many possible states, or that two distant objects can remain mysteriously connected*"? Yet these discoveries do more than challenge physics; they quietly unsettle the assumptions by which we ordinarily live. Superposition raises the unsettling possibility that what we perceive is not the whole of reality, but only the particular form reality takes when it comes into relation with our minds. Entanglement hints that separation itself may be less absolute than it appears – that beneath the apparent isolation of things there may exist a deeper connectedness. It is where we begin to ask not only what the world is, but who, or what, is looking at it.

The strangeness of quantum mechanics is not confined to laboratories. The very atoms that compose our bodies obey these principles. The electrons that form chemical bonds, the photons that strike our retinas, the protons in our DNA – all are quantum systems.

Imagine placing a ball at the bottom of a hill. In ordinary life, and according to classical physics, the ball can only reach the other side if it has enough energy to roll over the top. If it does not, it remains trapped where it is. Quantum particles, however, sometimes behave differently. They can occasionally appear on the far side of a barrier even though, by all the usual rules, they should not have had enough energy to cross it. It is as though the ball somehow passed through the hill instead of climbing over it. This strange behaviour became known as quantum tunnelling. At the smallest scales, particles do not exist as fixed objects at a single point, but as probability waves spread across space. Under certain conditions, part of that wave can leak through a barrier, allowing the particle to appear beyond it.

At the cellular level, quantum tunnelling allows reactions essential to life, such as enzyme activity and photosynthesis, to occur efficiently. But tunnelling is not the only strange quantum behaviour that appears to survive in living systems. Sometimes, tiny particles or waves can briefly remain coordinated, behaving less like separate pieces and more like parts of a single pattern. Physicists call this quantum coherence. Recent research suggests that such coherence may help birds sense the Earth's magnetic field during migration and may even play a subtle role in certain processes within the brain.

Thus, quantum mechanics is not an exotic abstraction but the fabric of our being. We are, in a literal sense, quantum creatures. Every thought, sensation, and breath arises from interactions that follow probabilistic rather than deterministic laws.

By the mid–20th century, quantum mechanics had revolutionised physics. Its predictions were confirmed to extraordinary precision. Technologies from semiconductors to lasers and MRI depend on it.

And yet, the theory left open the most unsettling question: what role does observation play in reality?

The so-called measurement problem asks: why does observation collapse the wavefunction? Does consciousness play a role? Or is collapse merely a physical interaction with measuring devices? Interpretations abound: The Copenhagen interpretation (Bohr, Heisenberg) holds that quantum states exist only as probabilities until measured.

The many-worlds interpretation (Everett) suggests all possibilities happen, in branching universes.

The pilot-wave theory (de Broglie–Bohm) posits hidden variables guided by deterministic waves.

Quantum mechanics introduced a profound disruption to classical thinking: particles exist in a superposition of states until measured, at which point the wavefunction "collapses" into a definite outcome.

But collapse into what?

And more intriguingly, collapse for whom?

Niels Bohr's response was the Copenhagen interpretation: *physics does not describe reality itself, but the outcomes of experiments we perform on it.* In Bohr's view, observation was integral to defining the properties of quantum systems. This is important.

Einstein found this intolerable. His retort – "*God does not play dice*" – encapsulated his rejection of a fundamentally probabilistic universe. He believed there must be hidden variables determining outcomes, even if they were beyond current detection.

Einstein remained deeply committed to an objective, mind–independent reality. He famously challenged Niels Bohr's Copenhagen interpretation of quantum mechanics, remarking:

"*I like to think that the moon is there even if I am not looking at it*".

For Einstein, physics described the world as it is, not as it appears through the act of measurement. This commitment led him to resist the quantum revolution's more radical implications.

The quantum revolution, for all its predictive success, left physics confronting the same kind of mystery expressed in the scriptures and spiritual texts.

Quantum physics transformed our picture of the universe from a predictable machine into a web of possibilities, correlations, and mysteries. It shattered determinism, challenged locality, and blurred the line between matter and mind.

Just as ancient myths spoke of chaos, void, and emergence, quantum mechanics spoke of uncertainty, probability, and collapse. Both point to a reality that resists final closure.

If light – one of the most fundamental phenomena in nature – behaves differently depending on whether it is observed, a deeper question naturally arises. What exactly is happening when observation takes place?

In the 1960s, Eugene Wigner advanced a provocative idea: c*onsciousness itself might be necessary to complete the measurement process.* His "Wigner's Friend" thought experiment extended Schrödinger's cat paradox – asking whether the collapse of the wavefunction depends on a conscious observer being aware of the outcome.

Wigner wrote:

"*It was not possible to formulate the laws of quantum mechanics in a fully consistent way without reference to consciousness.*"

This was a direct challenge to the assumption – shared by Einstein – that the observer could be abstracted away. Wigner instead suggested that awareness is fundamental, not derivative.

In everyday life, the world appears solid and definite. Objects seem to occupy precise positions. Events seem to unfold in a clear sequence. Yet at the most fundamental level, physics describes reality not as fixed objects but as evolving probabilities.

It is only when a measurement takes place that a particular outcome becomes definite.

This raises a question that has puzzled physicists for nearly a century. If reality at its deepest level exists as a cloud of possibilities, is what we perceive around us the result of a vast and continuous process of collapse?

Are the objects we see – the chair, the tree, the distant star – stable entities in their own right, or are they the visible outcomes of underlying quantum processes constantly resolving into definite states?

In other words, is the world we experience the universe as it truly exists, or is it the universe as it appears once possibilities have crystallised into events?

Physics does not yet provide a final answer.

Different interpretations of quantum theory offer different ways of understanding this strange transition from possibility to actuality. Some suggest that collapse is linked to measurement itself. Others propose that the universe evolves through multiple simultaneous realities.

Still others argue that collapse may simply be a feature of our description rather than a physical process.

Yet regardless of interpretation, one fact remains.

At the smallest scales known to science, the universe does not behave like a collection of solid objects moving through empty space.

If the universe at its most fundamental level is a field of possibilities, then the world we experience may not be reality as it is – but reality as it appears once those possibilities crystallise into events.

And from this field, the world we experience somehow emerges.

The double–slit experiment suggests something subtler: before measurement, the system exists in a "superposition" of possibilities described by a wave function. Measurement does not merely reveal a pre–existing property; it selects an outcome from a range of probabilities.

Again, we must be precise. Physics does not require human consciousness to collapse the wave function. Interaction with a measuring apparatus is sufficient. The key is that obtaining definite information alters the physical description.

This does not mean that human consciousness alters reality. What matters is interaction – the coupling of the photon with a measuring device. When path information becomes physically encoded in the environment, interference is lost.

Niels Bohr, one of the central architects of quantum theory, insisted that physics does not describe "how nature is" independent of observation. Rather, it describes *what we can say about nature within specific experimental contexts.*

The properties revealed depend on the arrangement of the measurement.

Albert Einstein was deeply uncomfortable with this. He believed that reality must possess definite properties independent of observation. The debate between Einstein and Bohr was not about theology. It was about realism. Notice what is being challenged. Consider this within the context of reality that we think we observe in everyday life? Can we be certain of what we are seeing? Is it "the" reality that our minds perceive, or is it one of the probabilities? A collapsed reality?

Does the world have definite properties before measurement?
Or are properties defined only in interaction?

The universe, at small scales, does not behave classically.

What, then, is light?

It is not simply a particle.
It is not simply a wave.
It is described by a quantum state – a probability amplitude that encodes potential outcomes.

Only when interaction occurs does a definite result appear.

Richard Feynman once remarked that the double–slit experiment contains "the only mystery" of quantum mechanics. Not because it is obscure, but because it reveals that nature does not conform to classical intuition.

At small scales, reality is not composed of tiny solid objects with fixed trajectories.

It is described by evolving possibilities.

Light is made of photons. Photons travel at the speed of light. According to relativity, as an object approaches light speed, time slows down relative to slower–moving observers. In the mathematical limit of light–speed motion, the interval along a light–like path becomes zero. Physics does not permit us to define a rest frame for a photon, so strictly speaking we cannot describe a photon's "experience." However, the spacetime interval along its path contains no proper time.

From our perspective, light may take one year, one million years, or ten billion years to travel. From the standpoint of spacetime geometry, there is no elapsed proper time along the photon's path between emission and absorption.

A photon leaves a distant star and is absorbed by your eye. For us, billions of years may have elapsed since that star emitted the light. But in the structure of spacetime itself, the emission and absorption are connected by a light–like interval with zero proper duration.

This does not mean time does not exist. It means that time is not absolute. It is not a universal river flowing uniformly for all. It depends on the structure of spacetime and on the motion of the observer within it.

So, what does it mean to say that time has passed?

It has passed for stars evolving, planets cooling, species emerging and going extinct. It has passed for observers embedded in spacetime moving at speeds slower than light. But the very carrier of information that allows us to see the universe – light – does not accumulate proper time along its journey.

Now pause and look again at what you call reality.

Every star sees every other star in its past. If there are beings somewhere else in this vast universe looking toward Earth, they are seeing ancient history. Perhaps dinosaurs. Perhaps even earlier life. Meanwhile, we look outward and see ancient galaxies. The entire cosmos is a web of delayed perception.

You have never seen anything as it is. You have only ever seen light that has already arrived.

Even the person sitting across from you is seen slightly in the past. Light must travel from their face to your eyes. Neural signals must travel through your optic nerve. Your brain must assemble the image. The "now" you experience is a stitched reconstruction of slightly outdated information.

Yet the mind insists: this is reality. This is present. This is solid.

If there is no universal present, if every observation is delayed, if the structure of spacetime itself denies a single shared now, then what exactly is the universe?

Is it a flowing river of time moving from past to future? Or is it a four–dimensional structure in which events simply are, and what we call the passage of time is a feature of how conscious beings navigate that structure?

We do not need to answer that yet.

We began with light because it seemed the simplest thing in the world. It illuminates, reveals, and allows us to see. Yet the deeper we looked, the stranger it became. Light proved not to be a steady stream, but a wave, a particle, a probability, and perhaps something beyond all such categories. With light comes distance, and with distance comes delay. Because light takes time to travel, every act of seeing is also an act of looking into the past. From this delay arise our notions of before and after, of past, present, and future. Time itself may begin not as something separate from light, but as a consequence of the way light moves through the universe.

From light emerged quantum theory; from quantum theory came superposition, entanglement, tunnelling, and the unsettling suggestion that reality is not as solid, separate, or definite as it appears. And yet these same strange principles do not remain confined to the microscopic world. They lie quietly within the atoms of our bodies, the chemistry of life, the processes of perception, and perhaps even the mysterious fact that anything is aware at all. What began as an enquiry into light has therefore already led us much further – toward the possibility that the universe, life, and consciousness are woven together far more deeply than we ordinarily imagine.

It is enough, for now, to recognise this: the reality we are certain of is mediated by light, structured by relativity, and assembled by perception. The present moment we defend so confidently is not a universal fact. It is a local interpretation.

ALL THAT MATTERS

Light, as we have seen, defines how the universe becomes visible to us. But light does more than illuminate matter; it is deeply intertwined with matter itself. Everything we call matter – whether it appears as a solid, a liquid, or a gas – is made of molecules. These molecules are themselves built from smaller units we know as atoms.

The word "atom" comes from the Greek atomos, meaning indivisible. Early philosophers such as Democritus proposed that all matter is made of such units. For centuries, this idea remained speculative.

In the early nineteenth century, John Dalton proposed the first modern atomic theory. Atoms were thought to be tiny, solid spheres – the ultimate building blocks of matter. That view did not survive long. In 1897, J. J. Thomson discovered the electron – a negatively charged particle far smaller than the atom itself. The atom was no longer indivisible.

In the early twentieth century, experiments began revealing the internal structure of the atom. Ernest Rutherford's gold foil experiment showed that atoms are mostly empty space, with a tiny, dense nucleus at the centre. Later, Niels Bohr refined the picture by suggesting that electrons occupy discrete energy levels around the nucleus. This was not entirely correct in its early planetary form, but it opened the door to quantum theory. The familiar image emerged: electrons orbiting a central nucleus, somewhat like planets around the Sun. The nucleus is, in turn, made of protons and neutrons. Protons, inside the nucleus, carry positive charge; electrons, as a hazy cloud overlapping the nucleus, carry negative charge; neutrons are electrically neutral. The positively charged nucleus attracts negatively charged electrons through the electromagnetic force. This is how an atom holds together, mostly.

Atoms rarely exist alone. Most of the time they combine with other atoms, forming structures known as molecules. These bonds occur because atoms interact through their outer electrons, linking together in stable arrangements. A molecule can be made of the same kind of atoms – such as oxygen molecules formed from two oxygen atoms – or it can combine different elements, such as hydrogen and oxygen joining together to form water.

The building blocks for these combinations are the elements listed in the periodic table. Each element represents a different kind of atom, defined by the number of protons in its nucleus. Hydrogen, carbon, oxygen, nitrogen, iron, calcium, gold – all the materials that make up the world around us come from these fundamental atomic types. And what is in the periodic table is all the matter that we know thus far.

When atoms combine in different ways, they create molecules with very different properties. Two hydrogen atoms and one atom of oxygen form water, a clear liquid essential for life. Rearrange those same atoms differently, and the substance would behave completely differently. Carbon atoms, arranged one way, produce soft graphite – the material in a pencil. Arrange the same atoms differently, and they form diamonds, one of the hardest materials known. From these combinations arise everything we see around us: rocks, oceans, air, plants, animals, and the human body. The enormous variety of matters in the universe emerges from the countless ways a relatively small set of elements can join together to form molecules.

Although the periodic table contains more than a hundred known elements, life is built from a remarkably small set of them. About 99% of the human body by mass is made from just six: *oxygen, carbon, hydrogen, nitrogen, calcium, and phosphorus.* Oxygen, carbon, hydrogen, and nitrogen alone account for about 96% of the body. Oxygen and hydrogen form the water that fills our cells; carbon provides the framework from which all organic molecules are built; calcium and phosphorus give structure to bone and teeth. Everything we call a body – flesh, blood, thought, and breath – emerges from the countless combinations of only a few basic atomic forms. In this sense, there is a curious resonance with the older idea, found in many traditions, that the body is made of only a handful of fundamental elements: earth, water, fire, air, and space. These were not elements in the modern chemical sense, but ways of describing the body's qualities – solidity, fluidity, warmth, movement, and the space within which all these arise. Different languages, perhaps, pointing toward the same underlying simplicity.

The atoms that make up our bodies did not originate with us. Long before the Earth existed, the universe was already manufacturing the elements that would one day become part of living beings. In the earliest moments after the Big Bang, only the lightest elements – mainly hydrogen and helium – were formed. Heavier elements came later, inside the immense furnaces of stars. Within their cores, nuclear reactions gradually forged carbon, oxygen, nitrogen, iron, and many other elements. When massive stars reached the end of their lives, they exploded in spectacular events known as supernovae, scattering these newly formed atoms across space. Over immense spans of time, this cosmic debris gathered into clouds, planets, oceans, and eventually living organisms. The carbon atoms in our cells, the calcium in our bones, and the iron flowing through our blood were once part of ancient stars that lived and died billions of years ago. The oxygen you breathe, the carbon in your cells, the hydrogen in your blood, the calcium in your bones – all are arrangements of atoms forged in ancient stars.

And these atoms do not truly "die." Atoms may rearrange themselves, bond with other atoms, break apart in chemical reactions, or even undergo nuclear decay in rare cases, transforming into different elements. But the fundamental particles themselves persist, constantly recycled through new forms. The atoms that compose your body today were once part of rocks, oceans, plants, animals, and stars. They have been borrowed temporarily by the body you call "yours," only to return again to the wider circulation of the universe.

In this sense, the body is not something we possess. It is a temporary gathering of ancient atoms that have been travelling through the universe for billions of years.

But it goes even further. Let's go deeper in the atom.

Protons and neutrons are not fundamental or absolute particles. They are composed of smaller constituents called quarks. Quarks are bound together by gluons – carriers of the strong nuclear force. This force is extraordinarily powerful at short distances, holding the nucleus together despite the electromagnetic repulsion between positively charged protons.

By the mid–twentieth century, physicists had assembled what is now known as the Standard Model of Particle Physics. It classifies the fundamental constituents of matter into two broad categories: fermions and bosons.

Fermions (The Bricks): These include Quarks and Leptons (like the electron). They make up the physical "stuff" of the universe.

Bosons (The Mortar): These are force–carrying particles. This includes the Photon (carries electromagnetism), the Gluon (strong force), and the Higgs Boson (which gives particles their mass).

Electrons belong to the lepton family. Quarks combine to form protons and neutrons. Bosons are force carriers. Photons carry electromagnetic forces. Gluons carry the strong force. W and Z bosons carry the weak nuclear force. The Higgs boson, confirmed experimentally in 2012 at CERN, is associated with the mechanism that gives certain particles mass.

What appears to be solid matter is, at fundamental scale, an intricate web of interacting quantum fields.

The positively charged nucleus attracts negatively charged electrons through the electromagnetic force. That attraction keeps electrons bound to atoms. The electromagnetic force arises from electric charge in the atom. Protons carry positive charge, electrons negative charge. Charges create electric fields – invisible regions of influence that extend through space. When opposite charges interact, the fields pull them together. This attraction keeps electrons bound to the nucleus and gives atoms their structure.

With the development of quantum mechanics by Werner Heisenberg and Erwin Schrödinger, the atom became stranger still. Electrons were no longer tiny orbiting planets. They were described by wave functions – probability distributions indicating where they were likely to be found (remember the double slit experiment? The wave function of photons?).

But atoms themselves can bond with other atoms through shared or transferred electrons. In covalent bonding, atoms share pairs of electrons. In ionic bonding, electrons are transferred, creating oppositely charged ions that attract one another. In metallic bonding, electrons move more freely among many atoms, creating conductivity.

When atoms bond, they form molecules. Carbon atoms bond in complex chains to form organic molecules. DNA, proteins, the molecules of your body – all are structured combinations of atoms bound by electromagnetic interaction. That is how things around you took shape. Everything is a molecular structure, a convenient bonding of atoms. No matter how shiny and cool a sports car appears to eyes, beneath it is just a well-arranged molecular structure. So are all the things around us. It is just the mind attached to things.

There is no glue in the classical sense. No miniature cement holding atoms together. There are only fields interacting according to quantum rules.

Temperature, pressure, solidity, liquidity – all arise from how atoms and molecules move and interact. Increase energy, and molecular bonds loosen. Decrease energy, and structure tightens.

At every scale, what appears stable is dynamic.

At the beginning of the twentieth century, Einstein's famous relation revealed that mass and energy are not separate substances but different expressions of the same underlying reality:

$$E = mc2$$

Energy can become matter, and matter can release energy. In the quantum world, this relationship appears in striking ways. When sufficiently energetic photons collide with matter, they can transform into particles such as electrons and their antimatter counterparts, positrons – a process known as pair production. In this sense, light does not merely travel through the universe; under the right conditions it can participate in the creation of matter itself.

Yet there is another puzzle hidden within this transformation. Einstein's equation seems to suggest that energy comes from mass. But photons – the particles of light – have no rest mass at all, and still, they carry energy. Einstein resolved this by showing that the energy of light arises not from mass, but from its frequency. The shorter the wavelength and the higher the frequency, the greater the energy carried by each photon. Blue light therefore carries more energy than red light; gamma rays vastly more still. In quantum theory, the energy of a photon is given by E = hf, where h is Planck's constant and f is the frequency of the light. A photon may be massless, yet because it is pure movement – pure oscillation – it still carries energy and momentum. Under the right conditions, *that energy can become matter*. The reverse also holds true. Sounds mysterious? Who said physics was boring?

A sufficiently energetic photon can give rise to an electron and a positron, as though vibration itself condenses into substance. Perhaps the deeper implication is that matter is not something fundamentally separate from light, but one of the forms that light can take. What does is mean for us?

Let's look a bit deeper.

Modern physics has revealed something even more surprising. Beneath the particles and forces we observe, it suggests that the universe is filled with invisible fields extending everywhere through space. There is an electron field, a photon field, and corresponding fields for every known form of matter and energy. These fields are not located in one place; they exist throughout the entire cosmos, even in what appears to us as empty space. What we call a "particle" is simply a local excitation in one of these fields – rather like a ripple arising on the surface of an otherwise still ocean. The particles we speak of – electrons, photons, and others – are not tiny solid objects moving through empty space. Instead, they appear to be small disturbances in invisible fields that permeate the entire universe.

In other words, space is not an empty and inert container holding celestial bodies. It is an interwoven, dynamic field that connects and interacts with everything within it. In modern quantum physics, particles are no longer viewed as tiny solid objects. They are understood as excitations – small disturbances – in underlying fields that permeate space. Similarly, an electron is not a miniature bead. It is a quantised excitation of the electron field. And a photon is an excitation of the electromagnetic field.

You might imagine these fields as a vast ocean spread everywhere. When the surface of the ocean ripples, we see waves. In a similar way, what we call a "particle" may simply be a ripple in one of these underlying fields. A photon is a ripple in the electromagnetic field. An electron is a ripple in another field associated with electrons. They are different ripples, yet they arise within the same deep ocean of reality. Though distinct, they are woven into the same fundamental fabric. Light and matter, therefore, are not strangers moving through separate realms. They are different expressions of a single quantum landscape – different patterns emerging from the same underlying structure of reality.

This realisation changes the way we think about the physical world. The body we inhabit, the air we breathe, the ground beneath our feet, and the stars scattered across the night sky are not collections of inert substances isolated from light. They are dynamic arrangements of energy, constantly interacting with photons streaming through the universe. Matter and light are participants in the same cosmic dance.

Fields, not objects, are primary in this description.

This leads to an unsettling realisation.

An atom is mostly empty space.

Quantum behaviour is not confined to laboratory particles or distant stars – it unfolds constantly inside the human body. We are also made of quantum particles – entities that, at their most fundamental description, exist as excitations of fields governed by probabilities. Each of the atoms in the human body contains electrons and nuclei that obey quantum laws.

At the microscopic scale:

Electrons exist in orbitals described by probability waves, not fixed paths.

Protons and neutrons are themselves quantum composites of quarks and gluons. Photons interact with biological molecules – from vision in the retina to photosynthesis in chloroplasts – with quantum efficiency.

Some researchers propose that quantum coherence may play a role in biological processes such as:

Olfaction through quantum tunnelling of electrons.
Photosynthesis via coherent energy transfer
Possible quantum states in the brain

This means the same wave–particle duality that governs a photon in deep space governs every photon absorbed by your eye, every electron in your synapses, every chemical bond in your DNA.

If consciousness interacts with quantum states – as Wigner suggested – then the arena of that interaction is not "out there" but also "in here", within every living cell.

And yet we experience ourselves as continuous, bounded, and definite.

The same electrons that behave as probability waves inside atoms somehow give rise to chairs, oceans, and human conversations that appear solid and definite. The chair beneath you feels solid. Your body feels continuous. The ground appears stable. For most of human history, matter was assumed to be composed of tiny, indivisible units – atoms – like miniature building blocks of reality. The physics governing the microscopic world does not resemble the physics governing everyday life – yet both are simultaneously true.

And yet, despite all this strangeness, you are still sitting in a chair.

The chair does not feel probabilistic.
It does not feel like a wave of possibilities.
It feels solid.

The wall in front of you feels impenetrable. The ground beneath your feet feels stable. The book in your hand does not dissolve into uncertainty. Yet the structure of atoms reveals something even more surprising.

An atom consists of a tiny central nucleus surrounded by electrons moving in regions around it. The nucleus contains most of the atom's mass, while the electrons occupy the surrounding space. But the scale of this structure is astonishing. The nucleus is extraordinarily small compared with the size of the atom itself.

If an atom were enlarged to the size of a large stadium, the nucleus would be no bigger than a small marble placed at the centre of the field. The electrons would occupy regions tens of metres away from that centre. Everything in between would be almost entirely empty.

This means that what we perceive as solid matter is, at the atomic level, mostly space. The solidity we experience arises not because atoms are packed like solid balls, but because the electromagnetic forces between atoms prevent them from passing through one another.

In other words, what feels like solid substance is actually the result of invisible forces acting across mostly empty space.

The physical world therefore appears far less compact and solid than our everyday experience suggests. What we call matter is a delicate arrangement of atomic structures – patterns of energy and force suspended within an immense amount of space.

In this sense, the solidity of the world is not a fundamental property of matter, but an effect produced by the interactions between atoms. Yet, we do not see it that way – we never see the world that way. We see buildings, parks, oceans, beautiful things, people, animals, flowers, the air we breathe in, the life we enjoy.

At this point a natural question arises. If everything around us – our bodies, the chair we sit on, the cup we hold – is made from atoms, and if atoms themselves are mostly empty space, why does the world feel so solid? Why can we hold a cup and sip tea without our hand passing through it? Why can we sit on a chair without sinking into it? Why can we not simply walk through walls?

The answer lies not in the solidity of atoms, but in the invisible forces that exist between them.

Atoms are surrounded by electrons, which carry negative electric charge. When the atoms in your hand approach the atoms in the cup, the electrons in those atoms begin to interact through electromagnetic forces. These forces strongly repel one another when the atoms come very close. This repulsion prevents the atoms from occupying the same space.

There is another quantum rule at work as well. Electrons obey a principle in physics that forbids two identical electrons from occupying exactly the same quantum state at the same time. In simple terms, the electrons in your hand cannot settle into the same configuration as the electrons in the cup or the chair. Nature simply does not allow it. In 1925, Wolfgang Pauli discovered it and termed it the "exclusion principle". It postulated that identical fermions – such as electrons – cannot occupy the same quantum state simultaneously. This prevents matter from collapsing into itself. It is one of the reasons white dwarf stars resist gravitational collapse. It is also one of the reasons your body does not sink through the floor.

Together, these electromagnetic interactions and quantum rules create what we experience as solidity. When you place a cup in your hand, trillions upon trillions of atoms are pushing back against one another through these invisible forces. Your hand does not pass through the cup for the same reason two powerful magnets cannot easily be pushed together at the same pole – the forces between them resist the overlap.

So, although atoms are mostly empty space, the interactions between their electrons form an invisible barrier that gives the world its firmness. What we experience as solid matter is therefore not the result of densely packed substance, but the effect of powerful forces acting between the particles of matter.

In this way, the solidity of the world is not a property of matter itself, but an emergent effect of the laws governing how atoms interact.

You do not "touch" the wall in the way you imagine. What you experience as touch is the resistance between electromagnetic fields surrounding atoms. The atoms never truly interpenetrate. The repulsive forces increase dramatically as the electron clouds approach each other, preventing collapse.

What feels solid is not matter pressing against matter.

It is force resisting force.

At a deeper level, quantum principles such as the Pauli exclusion principle reinforce this behaviour. Solidity is not a fundamental property of matter. It is an emergent effect of quantum fields interacting.

Now consider the states of matter.

Why is ice solid, water liquid, and steam gas?

The difference lies not in different kinds of atoms, but in how they are arranged and how much energy they possess. In solids, atoms vibrate in fixed positions within structured lattices. In liquids, they remain close but can move past one another. In gases, they move freely and are widely spaced.

Add energy, and structure loosens. Remove energy, and structure tightens.

What you call "solid," "liquid," and "gas" are simply patterns of motion and interaction at the atomic scale.

There is no solid essence hiding underneath.

There are only particles, fields, probabilities, and forces interacting according to mathematical laws.

And yet, we experience hardness, softness, temperature, pressure.

Where does that experience arise?

The world we experience is not built from solid cores. It is built from the behaviour of electrons.

And the electron, despite being described with extraordinary mathematical precision, remains conceptually elusive. It is neither classical particle nor classical wave. It is an excitation, a probability amplitude, a quantised disturbance in a field.

When we first realised that everything visible, tangible, and alive depends on the behaviour of something that cannot be visualised in classical terms, something shifted. The apparent solidity of the world began to feel less like substance and more like pattern.

The chair, the wall, the body, the brain – all are arrangements of electrons interacting through fields.

The world is not made of things.
It is made of behaviour.

At first glance, these ideas about atoms, quantum fields, and particles may seem distant from everyday experience – concepts belonging to laboratories, equations, and the abstract world of physics. But they are not distant at all. The same atoms, electrons, and invisible fields that govern stars and galaxies are also the very substance of our own bodies. Every cell, every nerve impulse, every breath we take is built from these same fundamental structures of matter. The body we inhabit is therefore not separate from the physical universe we have been describing. It is one of its most intricate arrangements – a living structure assembled from atoms forged in ancient stars and governed by the same quantum laws that shape the cosmos.

Seen from this perspective, the human body is not a special substance set apart from the rest of nature. It is the matter organised in a particular way – an extraordinarily complex pattern of molecules, atoms, and particles interacting according to the same laws that govern everything else in the universe.

And it is here that the question becomes more personal.

If the body is made from the same atoms as the world around us, what exactly is this body we call "ours"?

The scale of atoms within the human body is almost impossible to imagine. A typical adult human body contains on the order of seven octillion atoms – roughly – that's a 7 followed by 27 zeroes. That is a number so vast that even if you counted a billion atoms every second, it would take far longer than the age of the universe to count them all.

Yet these atoms are not uniquely ours.

Most of them have existed for billions of years, long before the Earth itself formed. As astrophysics has shown, many of the heavier elements in your body were forged in ancient stellar explosions. The hydrogen atoms in the water we drink were created in the earliest moments of the universe, only minutes after the Big Bang. Heavier elements – carbon, oxygen, nitrogen, calcium, iron – were forged much later in the cores of ancient stars. When those stars reached the end of their lives, many exploded in powerful supernovae, scattering these elements across space.

Over immense spans of time, this stellar debris drifted through interstellar clouds, eventually becoming part of new stars, planets, oceans, rocks, and living organisms. The carbon atoms in your cells, the calcium in your bones, and the iron circulating through your blood were once part of stars that lived and died billions of years ago.

Atoms themselves rarely vanish. They may rearrange, bond with new partners, break apart in chemical reactions, or slowly transform through radioactive decay. But the particles that compose them persist, continually recycled through new structures and new forms of matter.

In this sense, the body is not a completely new creation. It is a temporary gathering of ancient atoms that have travelled through the universe for unimaginable spans of time.

What we call a human body is therefore not a fixed object, but a momentary arrangement of matter that has been circulating through stars, planets, oceans, and living creatures long before our birth – and will continue long after we are gone.

Even the atoms in your body are constantly exchanging particles with the environment. The matter you call "yourself" is therefore not fixed. It is a pattern sustained through continual interaction with the world around you.

We experience reality through these interactions, detected by our senses. Sensory receptors respond to electromagnetic forces between atoms and convert these interactions into neural signals. The brain then assembles and interprets these signals as the familiar sensations of texture, resistance, weight, and solidity.

What feels like a solid and stable world is, in reality, the brain's interpretation of countless invisible interactions taking place between atoms. The solidity you experience is a translation.

There is no final solid layer.

Every layer dissolves into something subtler.

Every time we think we have found the foundation, it opens into deeper structure.

The chair you sit on is not solid substance.

It is a vast organisation of quantum fields, held together by forces, mostly empty space structured by interaction.

And yet, it feels firm. Yet, in real life, we have given things names, characteristics, and qualities. We will look deeply in the mechanics of the thinking mind and thoughts a bit later.

If the atom is mostly emptiness, and the solidity of matter arises from invisible forces and probability distributions, then what exactly is the world made of?

And if matter itself is structured energy patterns in fields, then what are you?

We are approaching the edge now.

But not yet stepping over it.

If matter itself is nothing more than patterns of energy unfolding within deeper fields, then the body we inhabit is also such a pattern – a temporary arrangement of atoms, molecules, and forces held together for a time. Yet this arrangement performs something extraordinary. Through the senses, it gathers signals from the world around it. Through the brain, it organises those signals into a coherent experience of reality. In this way the body becomes the instrument through which life is felt, perceived, and acted upon.

But the body is also something else. It gives us a boundary. A shape. A centre of reference from which the world appears to be observed. Because sensations arise within it, thoughts occur within its neural activity, and actions emerge through its movements, the mind gradually forms a simple and powerful assumption: this body is "me".

The same particles that gather into stone, metal, water, and trees also gather into living bodies. But in us, they seem to do more than merely exist. They begin to feel, to remember, to imagine, to ask. Out of matter arranged in a particular way arises the strange fact of human experience. We do not remain only rock, tree, or metal; we become aware of being. And with that awareness come questions that no atom, by itself, appears able to answer: What is it to be human? Why does anything experience at all? For what purpose does this vast universe give rise to beings who can wonder at their own existence? These questions will follow us from here onward.

And yet the body we call "mine" is itself a changing process – a shifting pattern of ancient atoms and interacting forces that has been assembled for a brief moment in the long history of the universe. It sustains life, enables perception, and anchors our experience of the world. But whether it truly constitutes the "self" we believe ourselves to be remains an open question.

To explore that question, we must now turn from the structure of matter to something more elusive: the way reality itself appears to us, and the mysterious presence of the one who seems to be observing it.

When bodily sensations, memories, and thoughts are gathered under a single linguistic marker – "I" – the grouping begins to feel like a stable entity. Yet beneath this conceptual overlay, nothing stands still. Everything remains in motion.

Even in the ordinary sense of time, we are never quite the same person we were a moment ago. The body is constantly exchanging matters with its environment. Neural activity shifts from second to second. Memories are updated, sensations arise and fade, emotions appear and dissolve. In the flowing continuity of time and space, what we call a person is always changing.

Yet the thinking mind tends to organise this movement into a narrative of continuity. Thoughts refer to past experiences, anticipate future possibilities, and weave them together into a story that appears to belong to a single, enduring subject. Because this narrative unfolds within language and memory, it creates the impression that there is a stable "I" moving through time and accumulating experiences.

But look more closely and the picture begins to shift. The sensations, thoughts, and perceptions that seem to belong to a separate observer are themselves the unfolding experience. The mind divides this flow into two – the one who experiences and the experience itself. From this division arises the familiar sense of a separate "me" living in a world of external objects.

Whether this division reflects the true structure of reality, or whether it is a construction of perception and thought, is a question we must now examine more carefully.

But thought presents continuity.

It assembles a narrative.
It selects snapshots from the stream and links them into a story.

The story becomes identity.
The world is not made of solid things.
It is made of interacting fields forming temporary patterns.

And among those patterns – you.

Despite his reluctance to accept the quantum role of the observer, Einstein expressed awe at the mystery underlying reality:

"The most beautiful and deepest experience a man can have is the sense of the mysterious" (Einstein, 1930).

He distinguished between the "intuitive mind" – a sacred gift – and the "rational mind" – a faithful servant, lamenting that modern society honours the servant and forgets the gift. These remarks suggest he sensed the importance of something beyond calculable physics, yet he did not weave it into his scientific models.

ALL THAT APPEARS

Step outside on any ordinary day and look around. The world appears vibrant, immediate, and unmistakably real. Streets hum with movement. Cars pass in steady streams. Neon signs flicker above cafés and restaurants. People walk briskly along sidewalks, speaking on phones, laughing with friends, carrying bags filled with the small necessities of life. Parks fill with families and children. Beaches stretch under open skies where waves rise and fall in a rhythm older than memory.

Cities glow at night with light and colour. Screens flash images and sound. Music spills from restaurants and nightclubs. Cruise ships glide across illuminated harbors. Stadiums erupt with cheering crowds. The air is thick with the aromas of food from distant cuisines, the sounds of conversation, engines, footsteps, laughter. Everywhere we look there are objects, events, technologies, city buzz, beautiful parks and landscapes, shopping centres, vibrant people and experiences that seem undeniably solid and immediate.

All of it feels unquestionably real.

Now imagine someone standing beside you, quietly suggesting that what you are seeing is not quite what it appears to be – that the solidity of the streets, the colours of the lights, the sounds of the city, even the sense of a stable world unfolding around you, may not reflect reality in the way you assume.

Most people would laugh.

The suggestion would sound absurd, perhaps even insulting to common sense. After all, the world seems plainly visible, tangible, and undeniable. We can touch it, walk through it, build things within it, experience it, and measure it with extraordinary precision. What could possibly be more real than the world directly before our eyes?

And yet, when we begin to examine how this experience of reality is formed, something unexpected starts to happen. The familiar solidity of the world begins to soften. The deeper we look, the more the foundations of what we call "reality" begin to shift.

Science would tell you that whatever you are seeing, every little thing, is inherently an atomic structure. Almost everything around us – the buildings, trees, oceans, food, clothing, and even our own bodies – is built from combinations of elements listed in the periodic table. These elements form atoms, which bond together to create molecules and complex molecular structures. From this relatively small set of building blocks the extraordinary diversity of the physical world arises.

At the first level lies physical reality, the one described by modern science. Here the universe appears as a vast system governed by mathematical laws – particles, forces, and energy interacting across space and time. Yet even this "solid" world turns out to be far less solid than it appears. Physics has revealed that atoms are almost entirely empty space. When you touch a wall, you are not experiencing matter colliding with matter in the classical sense. Instead, the electrons in the atoms of your hand repel the electrons in the atoms of the wall through electromagnetic forces. What feels like solidity is, in reality, a delicate balance of invisible interactions.

Yet the qualities we attach to these structures do not belong to the atoms themselves. The atoms in a flower do not contain beauty. The atoms in a storm do not contain danger. The atoms in a melody do not contain joy or sadness. These meanings arise in the mind that perceives them. Through perception, memory, culture, and language, the brain assigns characteristics to what it encounters – beautiful or ugly, pleasant or unpleasant, good or bad. In this way, the physical structure of the world and the meanings we experience within it are not the same thing.

And, what if what we think we are seeing is not everything that is out there?

Consider something as simple as the colour of leaves on a tree. We casually say that leaves are green, as if greenness were a property inherent in the leaf itself. But in physical terms, the leaf is not actually green.

Leaves contain molecules called chlorophyll that play a crucial role in photosynthesis – the process by which plants convert sunlight into chemical energy. Chlorophyll absorbs certain wavelengths of sunlight, particularly red and blue light, because those wavelengths drive the reactions needed for photosynthesis. The wavelengths that are not absorbed are reflected back into the environment.

Among those reflected wavelengths is the band of light that our eyes interpret as green.

When that reflected light reaches our eyes, specialised cells in the retina respond to those wavelengths and send signals to the brain. The brain then translates those signals into the colour we experience as green. The leaf itself contains no greenness as such. What it contains are molecules interacting with light according to the laws of physics. The colour emerges only when light, the eye, and the brain participate in the process together.

In this sense, the world is not filled with colours in the way we usually imagine. Colour is a translation – the brain's way of representing certain wavelengths of light.

The same principle applies to many of the colours we see in the natural world. Consider the blue of the sky. The sky itself is not painted blue. Sunlight reaching Earth contains all wavelengths of visible light. As this light passes through the atmosphere, molecules of air scatter the shorter wavelengths – particularly blue light – more strongly than the longer wavelengths. This process, known as Rayleigh scattering, spreads blue light across the sky in all directions. When that scattered light reaches our eyes, the brain interprets it as the familiar blue dome above us.

The ocean appears blue for related but slightly different reasons. Pure water absorbs longer wavelengths of light – especially red – more strongly than shorter wavelengths. The remaining blue light is scattered and reflected back toward our eyes. In addition, the ocean often reflects part of the blue sky above it, reinforcing the colour we perceive. Yet the water itself contains no inherent "blueness." What we see as blue is again the result of light interacting with matter and being interpreted by the visual system.

Many colours in nature arise not from pigments at all but from microscopic structures that interact with light in complex ways. The shimmering colours of butterfly wings, peacock feathers, and soap bubbles are examples of structural colour. Tiny structures on their surfaces bend, scatter, and interfere with light waves, producing brilliant colours that shift with the angle of observation.

In every case, colour is not a fixed property embedded in objects. It is the result of an interaction – light striking matter, reflected or scattered in particular ways, detected by the eye, and interpreted by the brain.

The world is not inherently filled with colour. It is filled with interactions that the mind translates into colour.

Even the way we see the world is not fixed. It develops gradually and varies widely across different forms of life.

A newborn baby does not experience the world in the same way an adult does. In the first weeks after birth, an infant's vision is still developing. The ability to distinguish colours is limited, contrast is more important than hue, and the world appears softer and less sharply defined. Only after several months does colour perception and visual clarity begin to approach that of an adult. What we now take for granted as a vivid and stable visual world is something the brain slowly learns to construct.

The situation becomes even more intriguing when we look at other species. Different animals perceive very different versions of the same physical environment. Many mammals, such as dogs, see a much narrower range of colours than humans, relying more on brightness and contrast. Some animals perceive the world largely in shades of grey. Birds, on the other hand, often see a broader spectrum of colours than we do, including ultraviolet wavelengths that are completely invisible to the human eye. To a bird, a flower or a feather may display patterns and signals that humans can never perceive.

Bees navigate using ultraviolet patterns on petals that guide them toward nectar. Certain snakes can detect infrared radiation, allowing them to sense the heat of prey even in darkness. Each species experiences a different slice of the same physical reality.

The world itself has not changed. What changes is the sensory system through which it is perceived.

In this sense, what we call "reality" is always partly shaped by the biological instruments through which it is experienced.

This raises an intriguing question.

What would happen if our senses suddenly changed? Suppose our eyes began to perceive the world in completely different colours and textures. The same trees, oceans, mountains, and faces would still exist, but their appearance would be altered by the way our visual system translated light. The colours we now associate with beauty or comfort might appear entirely different.

Would our sense of beauty remain the same?

Consider a flower we describe as beautiful because of its vivid colours. If our eyes perceived those wavelengths differently – if the red appeared dull or the green appeared grey – would the flower still seem beautiful to us? Or consider a sunset that fills the sky with warm shades of orange and gold. Much of the emotional response we feel arises from the colours we perceive. If those colours appeared entirely different, the experience itself might change.

Even something as simple as food illustrates this effect. The appearance of food strongly influences how we perceive its taste. When colours are altered artificially, people often report that familiar flavours seem strange or unpleasant. What we thought was a property of the food itself turns out to be partly shaped by the way our senses interpret it.

These examples suggest that many of the qualities we attach to the world – beautiful or ugly, pleasant or unpleasant – may not reside in objects themselves. They arise from the interaction between the external world and the sensory system that interprets it.

The structure of the world may remain the same, but the experience of it depends profoundly on how it is perceived. The world may remain unchanged, yet our experience of it could transform completely if the instruments of perception were different.

Beneath this lies what might be called perceptual reality – the world as constructed by the brain. Neuroscience increasingly suggests that the mind does not present the world exactly as it exists, but rather as it is useful for survival. The brain receives electrical signals from the senses and assembles them into a coherent picture of the world. Much of the physical universe –

ultraviolet radiation, radio waves, magnetic fields, and countless other phenomena – never enters our awareness at all. What we experience instead is a simplified representation shaped by millions of years of evolution. Cognitive scientists such as Anil Seth have described perception as a "controlled hallucination" – not meaning that the world is unreal, but that the brain actively constructs the experience we call reality – not a direct recording of reality, but a construction assembled by the brain.

If we look closely, something subtle begins to reveal itself.

The things around us simply exist in their own way. A tree stands. A stone rests on the ground. A cloud passes across the sky. At the level of their physical structure, these are arrangements of atoms and energy interacting according to natural laws. The tree does not contain beauty within its molecules. The stone does not contain ugliness. The sunset does not contain joy or sadness.

These qualities arise only when a mind encounters them.

Through perception, memory, and thought, the brain assigns meanings and characteristics to what it experiences. One person may look at a cloudy sky and feel calm. Another may see the same sky and feel melancholy. The physical scene remains the same, yet the experience of it changes because the mind interprets it differently.

Most of us move through the world as if reality were a solid, finished stage – a place where things such as trees, mountains, cities, structures, things, and people simply exist, waiting to be encountered. The world appears stable, self-contained, and complete. In many cases, we do not merely observe reality – we actively construct parts of it. Cities, institutions, technologies, and economic systems are not natural objects like mountains or rivers. They are creations of human thought, cooperation, and imagination, built and sustained through collective agreement and action. But when we begin to examine it more closely, layer by layer, that familiar picture begins to soften. What once seemed fixed starts to dissolve into something far more dynamic and mysterious.

In this way, the world we experience is not composed merely of objects, but of objects filtered through interpretation. The thinking mind attaches labels, evaluations, and emotions – beautiful or ugly, pleasant or unpleasant, desirable or undesirable. Gradually these interpretations become so familiar that we begin to assume they belong to the things themselves.

Even modern physics quietly undermines our confidence that we are seeing reality exactly as it exists in the present moment. Light, the very medium through which we perceive the world, takes time to travel. When you look at the moon, you are seeing it as it was about one second ago. When you look at the sun, the image reaching your eyes left the solar surface roughly eight minutes earlier. The light from distant stars may have travelled for hundreds, thousands, or even millions of years before arriving here. In other words, what appears before our eyes is not the universe as it exists now, but a stream of delayed information carried by light across space.

Even the objects closest to us are not perceived instantaneously. The light reflected from a friend's face, from a tree in the park, or from the cup in your hand requires a tiny fraction of time to reach your eyes and be processed by the brain. The delay is extremely small, but it is always present. Strictly speaking, we never encounter the universe in the exact moment of its occurrence. We encounter a continuous flow of slightly older signals, interpreted and assembled by the brain into what feels like the present.

The "now" we experience is therefore not a precise slice of reality, but a carefully constructed window assembled from incoming information. The world appears immediate and stable, yet what we perceive is always a little behind the unfolding universe itself.

When you look at someone across a room, the light reflecting from their face requires a small but measurable interval to reach your eyes. The delay is minuscule – fractions of a microsecond – but it exists. You are not seeing the person as they are at this exact instant. You are seeing them as they were a fraction of a moment ago. The scale becomes more dramatic when extended beyond the room. When astronomers observe the nearest star beyond the Sun, they are seeing light that left that star more than four years ago. Observations of distant galaxies reveal light that has travelled for millions or billions of years.

The night sky is not a live display of cosmic activity. It is a record of events long past. Thus, every visual perception is a delayed reconstruction. The world we experience is always slightly behind the events that produced it.

Consider a simple but astonishing possibility. Imagine a distant civilisation living on a planet millions of lightyears away from Earth. Suppose they possess powerful telescopes capable of observing our planet in great detail. The light leaving Earth today will take millions of years to reach them. But the light that is reaching them now began its journey millions of years ago.

If they were looking toward Earth at this moment, they would not see our cities, satellites, or modern civilisation. They would see the Earth as it was millions of years ago – vast forests, ancient oceans, and perhaps even dinosaurs roaming across the land.

Meanwhile, we are here, alive in the present, building cities, sending spacecraft into orbit, and looking out at the same universe.

From their perspective, dinosaurs still walk the Earth. From ours, they vanished sixty–six million years ago.

Both observations would be correct within the information available to each observer.

So which version is the real Earth?

The one we experience "Now"? Or the one they see through the light that has just arrived?

Physics suggests something remarkable: neither observer is seeing the Earth as it exists right now. Each is seeing a different slice of Earth's history carried through space by light. What we call "reality" is therefore inseparable from the information that reaches us and the time it takes to arrive.

The universe we perceive is not a perfectly simultaneous stage unfolding everywhere at once. It is a vast mosaic of moments, stitched together by travelling light.

Relativity deepens this conclusion. Because the speed of light is constant and finite, different observers in different states of motion will not agree on the ordering of distant events. What one observer calls "now" may not coincide with another's present. The physicist Carlo Rovelli has argued that reality is relational – that events are defined relative to interactions, not against a universal temporal backdrop.

The idea of a single, shared present dissolves under scrutiny.

When Einstein published his paper on Special Relativity, he began with a radical premise: the speed of light in a vacuum is the same for all observers, regardless of their motion.

This was not a poetic idea. It was a mathematical necessity emerging from Maxwell's equations of electromagnetism. Light propagates as an electromagnetic wave at a fixed speed. Classical intuition suggested that if one observer moved toward a beam of light, the measured speed should increase. If one moved away, it should decrease.

But experiments – most notably the Michelson-Morley experiment – failed to detect any such variation.

Einstein took this seriously.

He proposed that the speed of light is not relative. Instead, space and time themselves must adjust so that the speed of light remains constant.

This changed everything.

If the speed of light is invariant, then time cannot be absolute. Length cannot be absolute. Simultaneity cannot be absolute. Moving clocks tick more slowly. Moving rulers/measures contract. Observers disagree about what events occur "at the same time."

Space and time are not fixed containers within which events occur. They form a single structure – spacetime – whose geometry is intertwined with light.

So, what, then, is reality?

Across different cultures, thinkers and sages have long sensed that the world we experience may not be exactly what it appears to be.

In the Hindu philosophical tradition, this idea is expressed through the concept of Maya.

The Sanskrit word Maya is often translated as illusion, but the meaning is more subtle than simple deception. Maya does not suggest that the world does not exist at all. Rather, it points to the way reality appears to us through the filters of perception, language, and thought. What we experience is not the ultimate nature of things, but a conditioned appearance shaped by the mind.

According to the Upanishads and later Advaita Vedanta teachings, the world of forms – objects, identities, distinctions between subject and object – arises within this field of Maya. The tree appears separate from the sky, the body appears separate from the world, and the individual feels separate from everything else. Yet beneath these distinctions lies a deeper unity, referred to as Brahman, the underlying ground of existence.

Adi Shankaracharya, one of the most influential philosophers of Advaita Vedanta, illustrated Maya through simple analogies. In dim light, a rope may be mistaken for a snake. The snake appears vividly to the observer – fear arises, the heart races – yet the snake never truly existed. The misperception arose from the conditions of limited light and interpretation by the mind.

Similarly, the teachings suggest that much of what we take to be solid, separate, and permanent may arise from the way consciousness interprets experience.

This insight does not deny the practical reality of the world. We still walk on the ground, drink water, and feel the warmth of sunlight. But it raises a deeper question: how much of what we experience belongs to the world itself, and how much belongs to the structures through which we perceive it?

The intuition that reality may not be exactly as it appears is not unique to science or to any single philosophical tradition. Throughout cultures and centuries, thinkers have quietly arrived at similar suspicions about the nature of the world we perceive. In ancient Greece, Plato illustrated this through the famous allegory of the cave. Prisoners chained inside a dark cavern see only shadows cast upon a wall and believe those shadows to be the whole of reality. Only when one prisoner escapes and sees the world outside does he realise that what he had taken for reality was merely an appearance produced by deeper causes. In China, the Taoist philosopher Zhuangzi told a gentler but equally unsettling story. One night he dreamt he was a butterfly, fluttering freely through the air. When he awoke, he wondered whether he was a man who had dreamt of being a butterfly, or a butterfly now dreaming he was a man. The question was never meant to be answered; it simply loosened the certainty that our waking perceptions are the final measure of reality.

Similar reflections appear in other traditions. The Persian philosopher Ibn Sina imagined a "floating man," a person created fully conscious yet suspended in empty space, unable to see, hear, or touch anything. Even without sensory input, Ibn Sina argued, the person would still be aware of their own existence, suggesting that awareness itself may be more fundamental than the world it perceives. Christian mystic Meister Eckhart also hinted at this when he suggested that what we normally see are forms and distinctions created by the mind, while the deeper ground of reality lies beyond those conceptual divisions. In the Hindu tradition, the concept of Maya describes how the world appears through the conditioning of perception and thought, while Advaita philosophers such as Adi Shankaracharya used simple analogies–a rope mistaken for a snake in dim light–to illustrate how interpretation can transform appearance into conviction. Even in more recent times, sages like Ramana Maharshi returned to the same observation through the analogy of dreaming: just as a dream appears completely real while we are inside it, the waking world too appears unquestionable until we begin to investigate the nature of the one who is experiencing it.

Across these traditions, separated by geography and time, a similar insight quietly emerges. The world we experience may not be a fixed stage waiting outside us, but something that arises through the interaction between reality and the mind that perceives it. What we take to be solid and self–evident may be shaped, filtered, and interpreted in ways we rarely pause to examine.

More than two thousand years ago, the Buddha examined this very process with extraordinary clarity. Instead of asking what the world is made of, he asked how experience itself arises. His answer was expressed through a profound insight known as Dependent Origination – the principle that phenomena arise not independently, but through a web of conditions.

According to this insight, nothing appears in isolation. Experiences arise through chains of causes and conditions: contact between the senses and the world gives rise to sensation; sensation gives rise to feeling; feeling gives rise to craving, perception, and thought. What we call "the world" is therefore inseparable from the processes through which it is perceived and interpreted.

Reality, in this sense, is not a collection of independent things. It is a dynamic unfolding of relationships and conditions. In Buddhist teaching this process was described through twelve interconnected links – beginning with ignorance and conditioning, leading through perception, sensation, craving, and becoming, and ultimately giving rise to birth, ageing, and death. But the deeper insight is simple: experience is not the result of a single cause, nor the action of a permanent self. It is a dynamic unfolding of interdependent processes.

In its simplest expression, the Buddha described it in a single sentence:

When this exists, that arises. When this ceases, that ceases.

Nothing appears independently. Every phenomenon arises through a web of conditions.

A seed becomes a tree only through soil, water, sunlight, and time. A sound becomes meaningful only when vibrations in the air meet a functioning ear and a brain capable of interpreting them. Even a simple visual experience requires a chain of conditions – light reflecting from an object, travelling through space, entering the eye, triggering receptors in the retina, sending electrical signals to the brain, and being interpreted as an image.

Without any one of these conditions, the experience would not arise.

In this sense, what we call "the world" is not something that simply exists on its own, waiting to be perceived. It is an event that emerges through interaction between the external environment, the senses, and the interpreting mind.

The Buddha extended this insight even further. He observed that the process does not stop with perception. Once contact occurs between the senses and the world, a cascade of mental events follows.

Contact gives rise to sensation.
Sensation gives rise to feeling – pleasant, unpleasant, or neutral.
Feeling gives rise to craving or aversion.
Craving gives rise to attachment and identification.

Gradually, through this chain of conditions, the mind constructs a narrative: something is happening to me.

From that narrative emerges the familiar sense of a separate self – the feeling that there is an "I" standing inside experience, observing and reacting to the world.

Yet within the framework of Dependent Origination, this "I" is not an independent entity. It too arises through conditions – memory, sensation, perception, language, and thought.

The observer appears together with the observed.

Just as a wave arises through the movement of water, the sense of self arises through the movement of experience.

Seen in this way, reality is not a fixed stage populated by independent things and independent selves. It is a continuous process of arising conditions – light interacting with matter, senses interacting with signals, the mind interpreting patterns and weaving them into meaning.

Within this unfolding, the world appears, sensations arise, and the sense of "I" quietly forms.

But if both the world we experience and the self who experiences it arise through conditions, a deeper question naturally follows.

What, if anything, lies beneath this entire process of experience?

ALL THAT EXISTS

We live on this beautiful and abundant blue planet called Earth, the third planet orbiting our Sun. From the ground beneath our feet, everything appears calm, stable, and orderly. The rhythms of nature seem familiar and predictable – air that sustains us, forests and rivers that nourish ecosystems, mountains that appear immovable, and the intricate web of life that stretches from microscopic organisms to human civilisation. Within this environment, life unfolds in patterns that feel settled and secure, as if the world around us were a steady stage upon which our existence quietly plays out.

Yet this sense of stillness is largely an illusion of perspective.

In reality, nothing around us is truly stationary. At this very moment, the Earth is rotating on its axis at roughly 1,600 kilometres per hour at the equator. At the same time, the planet is racing around the Sun at nearly 108,000 kilometres per hour. The Sun itself, carrying the entire solar system with it, is orbiting the centre of the Milky Way galaxy at more than 800,000 kilometres per hour. And the Milky Way, one among hundreds of billions of galaxies, is moving through the expanding fabric of the universe.

We rarely notice any of this motion. The ground beneath us feels solid and unmoving. Trees stand quietly in the wind, cities remain where we built them, and the horizon appears steady. Yet in cosmic terms, we are passengers on a small rotating sphere travelling through space at extraordinary speeds.

To understand how small our place in the universe really is, it helps to step back and look at the scale of things.

The Earth, the entire world we know and inhabit, has a diameter of about 12,742 kilometres. To us, it feels vast. Crossing continents takes hours by aircraft and weeks by ship. Yet, compared with the objects surrounding it in space, Earth is remarkably small.

The Sun, the star at the centre of our solar system, has a diameter of roughly 1.39 million kilometres. More than one million Earths could fit inside the Sun.

And yet the Sun itself is only one object within the solar system. The solar system stretches far beyond the orbit of the outer planets. If we include the distant cloud of icy objects known as the Oort Cloud, the boundary of the Sun's gravitational influence may extend nearly 100,000 astronomical units from the Sun. One astronomical unit is the distance between Earth and the Sun – about 150 million kilometres.

Even this enormous region is tiny when placed within the next cosmic structure.

Our Sun is just one of roughly 100 to 400 billion stars in the Milky Way galaxy. This galaxy is a vast rotating disk of stars, gas, and dust stretching about 100,000 lightyears across. A single light–year – the distance light travels in one year – is about 9.46 trillion kilometres.

If our entire solar system were reduced to the size of a coin, the Milky Way would still be larger than the Earth itself.

And the Milky Way is not unique. It is only one galaxy among an immense population scattered throughout the observable universe. Current estimates suggest there may be around two trillion galaxies within the portion of the universe we can observe. Between these galaxies, there stretch unimaginable distances measured in millions and billions of lightyears.

The observable universe itself stretches roughly 93 billion lightyears in diameter.

Within this incomprehensible vastness are hundreds of billions of galaxies, each containing hundreds of billions of stars, many of which host planetary systems of their own.

Somewhere within one of those countless galaxies, around an ordinary star on the outer edge of a spiral arm, circles a small rocky planet called

Earth – the world upon which all human history has unfolded – every city built, every empire formed, every discovery made – occupies only a fleeting moment on a small planet orbiting an ordinary star.

And yet, despite this immense scale and motion, our experience of existence feels anchored within a narrow window of time and place. We wake, live our days, remember the past, anticipate the future, and measure our lives through the steady ticking of clocks and calendars. Time appears to move forward in a simple, linear flow – yesterday behind us, tomorrow ahead.

When we measure distances across the universe, we almost always measure them through time. Light from the Sun takes about eight minutes to reach Earth. Light from the nearest star takes more than four years to arrive. Light from distant galaxies may travel millions or billions of years before reaching us.

In this sense, distance itself becomes a measure of time. Life and age become a measure of time. The deeper we look into the universe, the further back in time we are seeing. Astronomers observing distant galaxies are not simply looking across space; they are looking into the past.

Time therefore becomes the invisible thread through which the universe reveals itself. It is time that stretches the universe into history – allowing stars to ignite, galaxies to form, planets to emerge, and life to evolve. Without time, distance would collapse and motion would have no meaning.

This profound relationship between existence and time was expressed in a striking way in the Bhagavad Gita. Standing on the battlefield of Kurukshetra, Arjuna asks Krishna to reveal his true cosmic nature. When Krishna manifests his universal form, overwhelming in scale and power, he declares:

कालोऽस्मि लोकक्षयकृत् प्रवृद्धो
लोकान्समाहर्तुमिह प्रवृत्तः

(Bhagavad Gita 11.32)

"*I am Time, the mighty force that brings worlds to their end.*"

In this moment, Krishna is not speaking as a human figure but as the cosmic principle through which all things arise, change, and pass away. Time becomes the great process within which creation unfolds and dissolves.

Ancient stories sometimes illustrated this mystery through simple yet powerful narratives. This ancient intuition – that time is not merely a backdrop to existence but its very engine – anticipates, in its own register, what modern physics would eventually confirm.

Long before Einstein, human cultures around the world were already wrestling with a disquieting possibility: that time does not flow at the same pace everywhere. Separated by geography and centuries, storytellers and sages returned again and again to the same strange theme.

One such story appears in the traditions surrounding the sage Narada, the wandering seeker known for his devotion and curiosity.

According to the story, Narada once asked Krishna about the nature of Maya, the mysterious power that shapes the world of appearances.

Krishna smiled, a playful glint in his eyes.

"Maya is not understood through words, Narada, but through the heart. But come, I am parched. There is a village just beyond that hill. Go and fetch me a glass of water, and then we shall speak of it."

Narada walked toward the village and knocked on the door of a house. A young woman answered. Struck by her beauty, Narada instantly forgot his purpose. As Narada spoke with her, time seemed to unfold in the ordinary way. He forgot the errand. He happily accepted when invited inside the home to have some food before travel and rest. Completely enchanted, he stayed to talk to her. One day turned into a week, and a week into a month. He spoke to her father, a farmer, and asked for her hand in marriage.

The wedding was celebrated with joy, and Narada settled into the life of a householder. He tilled the soil, built a sturdy home, and felt a deep sense of pride as his family grew. Three children were born to them, and Narada's days were filled with the laughter of his sons and the warmth of his wife's company. Twelve years passed like a golden dream; he was no longer a wandering sage, but a man of the earth, rooted in his love for his land and kin.

Then, one day a devastating flood swept through the region. The sky turned a bruised purple. A relentless monsoon broke over the valley, and the river nearby burst its banks. Within hours, the village was submerged. Narada gripped his wife's hand with one arm and held two of his children with the other, struggling against the rising torrent. The current was merciless. He watched in horror as his eldest son was swept away, then the younger two. He screamed in agony, reaching for them, but the water pulled his wife from his grasp as well. Suddenly, Narada was alone, tossed by the freezing waves, his entire world–twelve years of love, labour, and life–swallowed by the dark water.

"Help me!" he cried out, collapsing onto a patch of mud as the waters seemed to recede as quickly as they had come. "Lord, help me!"

"Narada?"

The voice was calm, almost cheerful. Narada looked up, shivering and gasping for air. He wasn't in a flooded valley; he was standing on the same parched road where he had started. The sun was still high, and the dust hadn't even settled. Krishna stood before him, looking exactly as he had moments before.

"Narada," Krishna asked gently, "where is my water? I have been waiting for nearly half an hour."

Narada fell at Krishna's feet, the phantom tears of twelve years still wet on his face. He finally understood. The life he had lived, the grief he had felt, and the attachments he had formed were all a flicker in the mind of the Divine–the perfect, overwhelming power of Maya.

The story is not meant to be taken as a literal account of time travel. Rather, it points to a deeper question: how real and stable is the flow of time we experience?

In the early Buddhist cosmology, existence is not confined to the human world alone. The Buddha described multiple lokas, or realms of existence, inhabited by different kinds of beings. What is striking in these descriptions is that time does not flow equally across these realms.

Buddhist texts mentioned that while in the human realm, a lifetime may span several decades, in certain heavenly realms, the passage of time may be vastly different. A single day in some deva realms may correspond to hundreds of human years. In other, even subtler realms of existence, time stretches further still. The Buddha used these descriptions not merely to speculate about invisible worlds but to illustrate something deeper: our sense of time is bound to the conditions of our existence.

Just as a fish experiences the ocean differently from a bird flying in the sky, beings existing in different conditions may experience time in ways that are not directly comparable. In this sense, the Buddhist cosmology suggests that time is not an absolute universal rhythm ticking identically everywhere. It is experienced relative to the structure of the realm in which life unfolds.

A similar theme appears in ancient Jewish and early Christian traditions through the mysterious figure of Enoch.

According to the Book of Genesis, Enoch was a righteous man who "*walked with God.*" Unlike others, whose lives ended in death, Enoch's story takes a different turn. The text simply says that he was taken by God.

Later writings, particularly the ancient text known as the Book of Enoch, expand this story in remarkable ways. In these accounts, Enoch is taken on a journey through the heavens, guided by angelic beings. He witnesses celestial realms, cosmic structures, and the movements of the stars.

During this journey, Enoch experiences events that seem to unfold over a significant period of time. He observes the workings of heaven, learns secrets of the cosmos, and records visions of the future.

Enoch was sent back to Earth for a period of thirty days to share his revelations before being taken into heaven forever. Yet when the story returns to the human world, the passage of time appears strangely compressed. Similar to the Krishna and Narada's story, some interpretations of Enoch's journey suggest that while he experienced ages of history and celestial mechanics in heaven, he returned to find his family and the world relatively unchanged from the moment he left, implying that heavenly time is so vast that centuries of human history pass in what feels like moments to the divine.

In Japanese folklore, the story of Urashima Tarō tells of a fisherman who rescues a turtle and is taken to an underwater palace beneath the sea. He spends what feels like only a few days in this beautiful realm. When he returns home, however, he discovers that hundreds of years have passed in the human world.

In Irish mythology in the tale of Oisín in Tír na nÓg, the "Land of Youth", Oisín travels to a mystical island where time seems to stand still. After what feels like a short stay, he returns to Ireland only to find that centuries have passed and the world he once knew has vanished.

A similar idea appears in ancient Hindu literature in the story of King

Kakudmi.

According to the Bhagavata Purana, King Kakudmi once travelled to the celestial realm of Brahma, the creator deity, accompanied by his daughter Revati. The king wished to seek Brahma's guidance in choosing a worthy husband for her.

When Kakudmi arrived, Brahma was listening to a celestial musical performance. The king waited patiently for the performance to finish before presenting his request.

After hearing the king's question, Brahma smiled gently and explained something astonishing.

During the brief time that Kakudmi had been waiting in the heavenly realm, many ages had already passed on Earth. Entire cycles of human history had unfolded. The kings whom Kakudmi had once considered as potential suitors for his daughter had long since disappeared, along with their kingdoms and civilisations.

When Kakudmi finally returned to Earth with his daughter, he discovered that the world he had known no longer existed. Vast spans of time had passed, and humanity had moved into a completely different age.

The story suggests that time in the realm of Brahma moves differently from time on Earth. What felt like a short interval in the celestial world corresponded to thousands of years in the human realm.

Across these cultures – separated by geography and time – a striking pattern appears. Human imagination repeatedly returns to the idea that time may not move at the same pace everywhere. The traditions do not require us to accept the physical existence of such realms in order to appreciate the insight they are pointing toward. Rather, they offer a way of thinking about time itself – suggesting that the passage of time may depend on the conditions under which experience unfolds.

These stories differ in detail, but they converge on a single unsettling intuition: that the flow of time experienced by living beings may depend on the conditions of the world they inhabit. Whether understood as mythology, symbolic teaching, or ancient cosmological speculation, they point toward a possibility that would eventually be confirmed – in a very different language – by modern physics. Time may not be a single universal river flowing identically for every observer. Instead, it may be woven into the very structure of existence, experienced differently depending on where – and perhaps what – we are.

Modern physics, surprisingly, arrives at a similar possibility through a very different path. Einstein's theory of relativity establishes that time does not flow at the same rate for all observers. Motion and gravity can cause clocks to tick differently in different regions of space.

Though separated by thousands of years and very different ways of thinking, both perspectives hint at the same unsettling possibility – that time may not be a single universal rhythm shared equally everywhere.

Physics can describe how time behaves and why it has an arrow for us, but it does not currently show purpose or intention behind it. The idea that time exists for life is a philosophical or spiritual interpretation, not a scientific result. What science does suggest is that the universe has a spacetime structure in which temporal order matters, and that the direction we experience as past > future is closely tied to entropy increasing from an unusually low–entropy early universe.

When talking about time, we are faced with three different questions:

First: why is there time at all in the equations of physics? In relativity, time is woven together with space into spacetime; it is not an add–on but part of the geometry within which events occur. Second: why do we experience a flow of time? That is partly a question of brains, memory, and perception. Third: why does time seem to have a direction – why do eggs break but not unbreak, why do we remember the past and not the future? That is the "arrow of time" problem, and the leading scientific explanation points to thermodynamics: entropy tends to increase, and this only works as an explanation because the early universe appears to have begun in a very low–entropy state.

Modern physics offers an important clue about why time appears to move in a single direction.

This clue comes from a concept known as entropy. We often measure distance by time because light takes time to travel, but in relativity space and time are part of one structure. There is no single universal "now" stretching across the cosmos, and clocks can run differently depending on motion and gravity. That means time is not a simple cosmic river flowing identically everywhere. But that still does not tell us why time exists. The strongest scientific answer at present is more modest: time is part of the structure of the universe we inhabit, and the arrow of time we experience seems to depend on special initial conditions – especially the low entropy of the early universe. Physicists and philosophers still debate why the early universe was so low in entropy; that part remains unresolved.

In simple terms, entropy describes the tendency of systems to move from order toward disorder. When a glass falls and shatters on the floor, the fragments scatter into many possible arrangements. Yet we never observe the reverse event – shards spontaneously gathering themselves into a perfect glass. When a drop of ink falls into water, it spreads outward and mixes with the liquid, but it never spontaneously gathers itself back into a single drop.

These everyday observations reflect a deeper physical principle known as the Second Law of Thermodynamics, which states that in an isolated system, entropy – the measure of disorder – tends to increase over time.

The universe itself appears to follow this rule.

Stars burn their fuel and eventually collapse. Mountains erode into sand. Structures decay. Living bodies age. Everywhere we look, processes seem to unfold in a direction that moves from more ordered states toward more disordered ones.

This gradual increase in entropy provides what physicists call the arrow of time – the reason we experience time as moving forward rather than backward. This one–way arrow is statistical, not fundamental. There are simply vastly more disordered states than ordered ones, so randomness itself drives time's apparent direction. But this is deeply unsatisfying, because it means time's arrow is emergent, not fundamental. The universe started in an extraordinarily low–entropy state – a "special" Big Bang – and has been unwinding ever since.

The theoretical physicist Sean Carroll has described this idea in simple terms. According to Carroll, *the reason time appears to flow in one direction is that the universe began in a remarkably low–entropy state shortly after the Big Bang*. Because there are vastly more ways for matter and energy to arrange themselves in disordered configurations than ordered ones, the universe naturally evolves toward increasing entropy. As Carroll puts it, there is simply "much more room for disorder to grow."

From this perspective, the passage of time may not be a mysterious force pushing events forward. Instead, what we experience as time flowing may be the natural consequence of the universe gradually exploring more and more possible configurations of matter and energy.

The physicist John Archibald Wheeler expressed the mystery of time in a different way. Wheeler often emphasised that the *universe is not merely a static collection of objects but a dynamic process in which events unfold and give meaning to one another.* He famously suggested that time and the universe are inseparable, and that the structure of reality may emerge through the unfolding of events themselves.

Seen from this perspective, time is not just a clock measuring change. It is deeply connected to the processes that allow change to occur at all.

Entropy gives this process direction.

Without the gradual increase of entropy, the universe would have no preferred direction of change. Eggs could unscramble themselves. Heat could spontaneously flow from cold to hot. Memories could form equally well of the future as of the past.

But in the universe that we inhabit, entropy increases, and that increase quietly shapes the direction of time.

It is this subtle imbalance – this movement from order toward greater disorder – that gives us the sense that time is always moving forward.

Einstein's relativity shattered the Newtonian clock. In his equations, time is not a universal river flowing at the same rate for everyone – it is elastic. It is not a universal constant but a flexible dimension that stretches or compresses based on speed and gravity. A clock on a satellite ticks faster than one on Earth. These effects are not just theoretical but are measured daily; for instance, GPS satellites move so fast and are so far from Earth's gravity that their onboard atomic clocks must be manually corrected by about 38 microseconds a day to stay synchronised with clocks on the ground. A twin who travels near the speed of light returns younger than her sibling. Time, in this view, is just another dimension of spacetime – not a flowing process, but a geometry. space and time are inextricably linked into a single four–dimensional fabric called spacetime, and because the speed of light must remain the same for everyone, time itself has to adjust to compensate for motion.

This is deeply strange because it implies that the future already exists. Your death, and everything after it, is already "there" in the block – you just haven't reached that coordinate yet.

General Relativity adds another layer by explaining that massive objects like planets and stars warp the very fabric of spacetime like a heavy ball on a trampoline. This warping causes gravitational time dilation, meaning time actually ticks slower in stronger gravitational fields, such as at sea level compared to the top of a mountain or near the intense pull of a black hole.

Hermann Minkowski, Einstein's former mathematics teacher, reformulated relativity by describing space and time as a single four–dimensional entity: spacetime. Events are not arranged in a flowing river but positioned within a geometric structure. Past and future are not annihilated; they are coordinates. The present moment has no special status in the equations. It simply is.

The "block universe" view tells us that past, present, and future coexist within spacetime, and that the sensation of temporal flow arises from how conscious beings traverse this structure.

The block universe theory, or eternalism, posits that our universe is a giant, four–dimensional "block" where all points in time–past, present, and future–exist simultaneously and are equally real. In this view, your birth, your current actions, and even your death are already encoded at specific coordinates within the fabric of spacetime. This model treats the dimension of time much like a dimension of space; just as Paris and New York both exist even if you are only in one of them, the years 1920 and 2124 are "already there" in the block, even if you are not currently experiencing them.

The theory suggests that the "flow" of time is a persistent illusion created by human consciousness as it moves along its "world line"–a unique path through the block. We perceive a moving "now" because our brains process information sequentially, but from an outside perspective, the universe is a static, unchanging structure where every event is fixed like a frame in a completed film. This implies a deterministic reality where the future is as unchangeable as the past, raising profound questions about free will.

While this view aligns closely with the mathematics of theory of relativity–which shows that different observers can disagree on what is "happening now"–it faces significant challenges from quantum mechanics, where the future is often seen as a realm of undetermined probabilities rather than a fixed landscape. Some thinkers propose an alternative called the "growing block universe," where the past and present are real, but the future is not yet written, coming into existence only as the edge of the "now" advances.

Science can describe time, measure it, and reveal that it flows differently under different conditions. But when we ask why time exists at all, or why the universe began in a state that allows history, complexity, and life to unfold, physics grows quiet. At that edge, explanation gives way to wonder.

At this point, a deeper question begins to emerge.

Time seems obvious to us because we live within it. We remember the past, experience the present, and anticipate the future. Photographs of our lives appear to confirm this passage: a picture taken when we were eighteen and another when we are forty–five tells a story of years that have unfolded between those moments. The photograph itself does not contain time. The younger and older faces simply exist as two different arrangements of matter captured at different moments. It is the mind that links them together, constructing a narrative of change and duration.

The question then becomes unavoidable: for whom does time pass? And what exactly is passing?

A leaf moves through time – it exists at t=0 green and high, at t=5 yellow and falling, at t=10 crumbled on the ground. In quantum physics, the leaf is all of those states simultaneously, laid out in the block universe like frames in a film reel. What moves is your consciousness – your point of experience scanning across those frames.

The Buddhists call ordinary time consciousness saṃsāra – the wheel of conditioned arising, where each moment causes the next in an endless chain – reality as a continuous arising and passing of phenomena. The Hindu concept of māyā is not that the world doesn't exist – it is that its apparent solidity and linear unfolding is a projection of awareness, not the bedrock reality. Sensations arise, persist briefly, and fade. Thoughts appear and disappear. Emotions emerge and dissolve. From this perspective, what we experience as the passage of time may simply be the mind observing this ongoing process of arising and vanishing events.

Liberation is not escaping time but seeing through the story the mind constructs about it. Without memory, comparison, and awareness, would time appear in the same way?

Relativity shows us that time is elastic. But at one extreme – the extreme of light itself – the elasticity becomes absolute, and time does not merely slow. It stops. Consider a photon – a particle of light, massless and sovereign. It travels at the only speed available to it: c, the cosmic speed limit, 299,792 kilometres per second. And here the equations of relativity deliver their most vertiginous result.

For any object with mass, moving faster causes time to dilate – clocks slow, intervals compress. As you approach the speed of light, time slows toward zero. The photon, having no mass, does not approach this limit – it is this limit. It cannot travel at any other speed. And so, the time dilation formula, applied to a photon, does not merely slow its clock. It stops it entirely.

From within the photon's frame of reference – if such a thing can even be said to exist – the interval between emission and absorption is precisely zero. A photon released from a star in a galaxy two billion lightyears away, absorbed by your retina on a Tuesday afternoon, has experienced no duration whatsoever between those two events. In its own geometry, they are the same moment. The entire journey – across two billion years of what we call time, across an unimaginable gulf of what we call space – collapses into a single, dimensionless point.

The photon does not travel. It simply is – simultaneously at its source and at its destination, with nothing in between.

This is not poetry. The mathematics insists on it. And yet it tears at something deep in our intuition, because we who receive that light do experience the two billion years. The star may no longer exist. Civilisations may have risen and fallen in the galaxy it came from. The photon carries no memory of the journey, because for the photon, there was no journey. Only a single, eternal instant of contact – emission indistinguishable from arrival.

In this sense, light does not merely illuminate the universe. It stitches it together across time. Every photon that reaches your eye is a thread connecting your present moment directly to a distant past – not as a metaphor, but as a geometric fact. The photon is the universe's way of making two moments one.

And if you allow yourself to sit with that – the idea that the light pouring through your window this morning left its source perhaps eight minutes ago, perhaps eight million years ago, and arrived having experienced nothing in between – then the mystic's claim that time is an illusion begins to feel less like surrender and more like precision.

If even the carrier of time does not live within time, what exactly is the "timeline" we defend so confidently?

If this is difficult to imagine, it is because our everyday experience is anchored within a very narrow range of speeds and conditions.

Relativity unsettles our picture of time at the scale of the very large and the very fast. Quantum mechanics approaches from the opposite direction – and the strangeness it reveals is of a different kind entirely. The electron, as we saw, lives in superposition – a ghost of probabilities haunting several possible states at once, committing to one only under the pressure of observation. The photon behaves analogously but adds a further strangeness: it carries no internal clock. Where the electron's uncertainty is about position, the photon's is about time itself. Both point toward the same unsettling conclusion – that at the foundation of reality, the crisp coordinates of here-and-now dissolve into something far more ambiguous. Philosophers like Eugene Wigner and John von Neumann argued that consciousness may be essential to this collapse, making observation not just a passive act but a participatory one. In that case, time itself is not merely "out there" but inseparably tied to awareness.

The matter that forms our bodies is built from these same quantum ingredients – atoms, electrons, and fields interacting according to quantum laws. Yet the world we experience appears solid, stable, and continuous.

What exactly bridges the gap between the strange quantum behaviour of the microscopic world and the stable reality we experience at human scales remains one of the deepest questions in physics.

Then there is the phenomenon of quantum entanglement, in which two particles that interact can remain correlated across vast distances. A measurement performed on one immediately determines the state of the other, even when separated by enormous spans of space. Entanglement does not imply multiple universes or parallel copies of everything in any simple sense, but it does reveal that the universe may be far more deeply interconnected than our everyday perception suggests.

When these scientific insights are placed alongside philosophical and spiritual traditions, a profound question begins to emerge.

If consciousness or awareness is not merely a by–product of the brain but something more fundamental – as many spiritual teachings propose – could it exist outside the framework of time that structures physical events?

And if our deepest identity is not the body or the stream of thoughts that arise within it, might the sense of time itself belong only to the changing phenomena we observe, rather than to the awareness that observes them?

These questions do not yet have definitive answers.

But they point toward a possibility that has fascinated philosophers, physicists, and contemplatives alike: that the reality we experience may be only one layer of a much deeper structure – a structure in which time, identity, and the world itself may appear very differently from how they seem in the ordinary flow of daily life.

Light defines the limits of causality. Nothing outruns it. Nothing transmits information faster. It binds space and time together. It creates the structure within which we speak of past and future.

And yet, in its own mathematical description, it does not "move through time" the way massive objects do. From our perspective, light travels across immense distances. From the geometry of spacetime itself, the interval along its path contains no experienced duration.

If what carries information through the universe does not itself inhabit time in the way we do – if its behaviour depends on interaction – then what exactly is the nature of the "timeline" we defend so confidently?

Our sense of past and future is built on delayed light.
Our sense of distance is built on finite light speed.
Our historical memory is built on light arriving.
Our biological perception is built on photons striking retinal cells.

The entire visible world is a delayed interpretation of electromagnetic interaction.

And the phenomenon that generates that delay does not accumulate duration.

Light shapes our experience of time.
But in its own description, time collapses.

If even time is not what it seems, what becomes of the story we tell about our lives?

Roger Penrose has explored deep tensions in our understanding of time, suggesting that the flow we experience may not correspond directly to the mathematical structure of the universe. While he does not dismiss time outright, he questions simplistic interpretations of temporal flow. In his investigations into the deep structure of the universe, he has suggested that our ordinary experience of time may not correspond directly to the fundamental description provided by physics. The mathematics does not contain a moving present. It contains relations between events.

From the standpoint of spacetime geometry, there is no privileged "now" sweeping across the cosmos. The mathematics of relativity does not privilege a single cosmic "now." Events are ordered by relation, not by a universal present sweeping across space.

There are events.
There are relations.
There is structure.

The sensation of time flowing – of moments passing – may arise not from the external world itself, but from the way biological systems process change.

If the geometry of spacetime contains no moving present, then what becomes of the felt passage of time?

Again, the mathematics of relativity does not contain a privileged present sweeping across the cosmos. It contains relations between events. If physics provides the structure, psychology provides the animation.

The equations describe a spacetime block – events arranged in relation.
But the human nervous system behaves like a projector moving through that film strip, illuminating one frame at a time.

The sensation of flow may not belong to spacetime itself, but to the biological mechanism scanning it.

But the human mind insists on flow.

Physics questions the structure of time. Philosophy questions whether the present can even be grasped. Contemplative traditions question something subtler: whether the felt flow of time is partly a construction of mind. These approaches are not identical, and they should not be confused. Yet they converge on a shared destabilisation – the "now" we live inside may not be the clean, universal river we imagine.

Centuries before Einstein, St. Augustine wrestled with the same puzzle. In his Confessions, he asked: *What is time? If no one asks me, I know. If I wish to explain it, I do not know.* He observed that the past no longer exists, and the future does not yet exist. Only the present appears real – yet even the present cannot be grasped, because the moment we attempt to capture it, it has already passed.

He concluded that past and future exist only in the mind: the past as memory, the future as expectation.

Time, then, becomes psychological.

Long before relativity, sages questioned the reality of temporal flow. In the Upanishads, time is described as a manifestation within Brahman – not ultimate reality. In the Bhagavad Gita, Krishna speaks of the eternal Self as unborn, undying, beyond temporal change. The Self is not within time; time appears within it.

J. Krishnamurti would later echo something similar, though from a different angle. He spoke of psychological time – the movement of thought projecting itself into "what was" and "what should be." For him, chronological time – the time of clocks and physical processes – is necessary. But psychological time – the narrative constructed by memory and anticipation – is the root of inner conflict.

Buddhist teachings similarly dismantle temporal solidity. Nagarjuna, in the Mūlamadhyamakakārikā, analysed past, present, and future and concluded that none possess inherent existence. The present cannot be grasped, the past is gone, the future not yet arisen. Time dissolves under analysis.

Zen masters spoke of "suchness" – reality as it is before conceptual division into before and after. Dōgen, the 13th–century Zen teacher, wrote in Uji ("Being–Time") that each moment is complete in itself, not a fragment moving from past to future but an expression of total reality.

Sufi mystics likewise described eternity not as endless duration but as the absence of temporal separation – the timeless now.

From the physicist's chalkboard and the mystic's meditation cushion, a similar destabilisation emerges.

Time may not be what it appears to be.
And yet – our entire psychological structure depends on it.
Memory creates past.
Anticipation creates future.
Narrative stitches them together.

Light gives us delay.
Biology gives us sequence.
Thought gives us storyline.
Together they create what we call a life journey.

But if the fundamental structure of reality does not contain a moving present…

If the carrier of information does not accumulate time…
If the geometry contains relations rather than flow…
Then perhaps what we call time is a feature of perception – not the property of the universe itself.

This does not deny clocks.
It does not deny ageing.
It does not deny causality.

It simply loosens the certainty with which we defend a linear story.

Even psychologically, the sense of present identity depends on continuity across moments. Memory carries forward prior states. Expectation projects possible futures. The present is never pure immediacy. It is always a convergence of retention and anticipation.

This does not make it unreal.

It makes it constructed.

The immediate feeling of being here, in this moment, is already the outcome of integration – physical, neurological, and psychological.

When we say, "this is happening now," we are referring to a model – a stabilised frame generated by a living system moving through spacetime. The certainty of "now" rests upon a construction that is never directly perceived.

None of this implies that reality is illusion. Rather, it reveals that intuitive certainty does not equate to fundamental truth. The present, as commonly conceived, is not a universal property of the cosmos. It is a local phenomenon – a way of organising information within a living system. If every perception is delayed, if simultaneity is relative, and if the present is assembled rather than given, then a subtle but important question emerges:

The enquiry does not begin in abstraction.

It begins here – in the simple fact that something is aware of this moment.

Before past.
Before future.

What, exactly, is present?

Einstein showed that time is not absolute; quantum mechanics shows that reality is not fixed until observed. Yet physics still struggles with integrating the one element that experiences time and observation – consciousness itself.

John von Neumann, in his Mathematical Foundations of Quantum Mechanics (1932), made the bold claim that the chain of measurement cannot terminate within physics itself. A measuring device is still physical, subject to the same rules. Therefore, the chain ends only at the conscious observer.

Eugene Wigner took this further, arguing that *without consciousness there is no collapse of the wave function.* To him, physics without consciousness was incomplete. This was a radical move, challenging the core materialist assumptions of science. Yet this idea remained too controversial. Physicists largely dismissed it, preferring interpretations like the "many worlds" or "hidden variables" that avoided bringing consciousness into the picture.

Consciousness became the "elephant in the laboratory," present in every act of observation, yet excluded from the theory.

To explore the nature of reality without including consciousness is like trying to understand a novel by examining only the ink and paper, ignoring the act of reading. The future is not a line waiting to be walked–it is a branching cloud, crystallising only when consciousness looks.

If time itself is an illusion, then the question naturally arises: illusion for whom? For whom does this "flow" of time appear so real, when physics at its deepest level suggests otherwise?

Physics questions the structure of time. Philosophy questions whether the present can even be grasped. Contemplative traditions question something subtler still: whether the felt flow of time is partly a construction of mind. These approaches are not identical, and they should not be confused. Yet they converge on a shared destabilisation – the "now" we live inside may not be the clean, universal river we imagine.

It is here that we stumble upon a gap in modern science. Physics, for all its extraordinary power, has largely proceeded as though the observer–the conscious experiencer–could be set aside. Equations describe trajectories, probabilities, and fields, but not the awareness that beholds them. Einstein, Wigner, von Neumann, and many others danced on the edges of this realisation, but few were able–or willing–to take the decisive step: to consider consciousness as more than a by–product of matter.

We began with motion – the invisible speeds at which this apparently still planet hurtles through space. We followed the thread through the night sky, where the light reaching your eye was emitted before your grandparents were born. We watched time dilate under speed and gravity, collapse entirely for the photon, and dissolve under the scrutiny of quantum observation. We sat with the mystics who reached similar conclusions through a different path – not equations but silence, attention, and the direct inspection of experience.

What emerges, across all these approaches, is not a single answer but a consistent loosening. The certainties we carry – that time flows forward, that now is universal, that the past is gone and the future is waiting – are revealed as local, constructed, contingent on the conditions of the observer.

Entropy gives time a direction. Light gives time its reach. Memory gives time its texture. Together they create what we call a life journey. But if the fundamental structure of reality does not contain a moving present, if the carrier of information does not accumulate duration, if the geometry contains relations rather than flow – then perhaps what we call time is a feature of perception, not a property of the universe itself.

And if that is so, then the most interesting question is not what time is, but who is doing the experiencing. Not the equations, not the photon, not the entropy gradient – but the awareness that reads all of these as a story, that stitches past and future into the living fabric of a life.

That awareness is where physics grows quiet. And where everything interesting begins.

PART II: THE CONSTRUCTED MIND

THE BEGINNING

When we look up at the night sky, we are not only witnesses to beauty but also to immensity. The observable universe spans an estimated 93 billion light years in diameter, containing hundreds of billions of galaxies, each with billions of stars, many with their own planetary systems. Our Earth is a speck orbiting one modest star in an outer arm of the Milky Way galaxy, which itself is only one of billions of spiral galaxies suspended in an ever–expanding cosmos. This scale humbles our sense of importance: if the universe were reduced to the size of Earth, our entire solar system would be smaller than a pinhead.

Yet human cultures across time have insisted on asking: *Why* does all this exist? What lies behind the stars, the galaxies, and the fabric of space–time? This drive to seek origins and meaning has been a cross–cultural constant. It is from this awe and humility that myth, philosophy, and science all arise.

Long before the language of physics was born, human beings sought patterns in the dance of stars, the fall of stones, and the mysterious motions of rivers. In ancient Greece, thinkers from Heraclitus to Aristotle asked what lay behind appearances – whether it was flux, number, purpose, or the void. Democritus imagined indivisible atoms; Plato sought eternal forms behind the visible world; Aristotle provided a comprehensive, rational cosmos in which everything had its place. These were not scientific theories in the modern sense. They were attempts to think clearly about a universe that appeared, at once, to be ordered and inexplicable.

That tradition passed through the Islamic Golden Age – where scholars like Ibn Sina, Alhazen, and Averroes preserved, critiqued, and extended Greek thought, adding empirical rigour and original insight – and returned to medieval Europe transformed. By the time of Thomas Aquinas, the cosmos was a rational hierarchy ordered under God. But seeds of change were already present. The question was no longer only what the universe was made of, but how it actually moved – and whether its laws could be measured, not merely reasoned about.

The Renaissance and early modern period brought radical upheavals. Nicolaus Copernicus (1473–1543) proposed heliocentrism, displacing Earth from the cosmic centre. This was more than astronomy; it challenged theological and philosophical assumptions of humanity's privileged place.

Johannes Kepler (1571–1630), influenced by Pythagorean harmonies, discovered that planets move in ellipses, not circles. His three laws of planetary motion offered mathematical precision to the heavens.

Galileo Galilei (1564–1642), armed with the telescope, observed mountains on the moon, moons of Jupiter, and phases of Venus – demolishing Aristotelian perfection of the heavens. More importantly, Galileo championed experimentation: dropping bodies to test motion, quantifying acceleration. In his writings, he declared that nature is written in the language of mathematics.

It was Galileo who first broke decisively from Aristotle's static cosmos. In his study of falling bodies, he stripped motion of "purpose" and sought instead its measurable regularity. A ball rolling down an inclined plane did not fall faster because it "desired" the earth, but because acceleration followed a law. Galileo's telescope revealed a moving universe, moons circling Jupiter, imperfections on the sun, and thus shattered the perfection of Aristotle's heavens. The cosmos was no longer a fixed hierarchy, but a dynamic system governed by laws discoverable to human reason.

Descartes (1596–1650), building on the Scientific Revolution, envisioned a mechanistic universe governed by laws of motion. For him, the cosmos was like a clockwork, a system that could be fully explained by matter and motion – with God as the initial designer. While Aristotle's cosmos was teleological (purpose–driven), Descartes' was mechanical (law–driven).

By the early 17th century, natural philosophy had shifted decisively. Observation, mathematics, and experiment were now the keys to knowledge. Yet the framework was incomplete. How did motion operate universally? Why do planets follow Kepler's laws? What is the connection between terrestrial falling apples and celestial orbiting moons? The stage was set for Isaac Newton (1642–1727). His Principia Mathematica would unite terrestrial and celestial mechanics, bringing coherence to two millennia of fragmented speculation. The clockwork cosmos was about to be born.

Isaac Newton brought this search for order to its triumph. With his Philosophiæ Naturalis Principia Mathematica (1687), he unified the heavens and the earth. The apple that fell in his orchard obeyed the same law of gravitation that held the moon in orbit. Suddenly, the cosmos could be envisioned as a grand machine – vast, intricate, and precise.

Newton's cosmos was not merely mathematical but mechanical. The metaphor of a "clockwork universe" soon gained popularity. Just as a clock, once wound, runs predictably according to its gears and springs, so too the universe runs according to deterministic laws. Every motion, every event, could in principle be predicted if initial conditions were known.

In the Newtonian vision, the cosmos was deterministic. In Newton's vision, God was the great architect who set the gears in motion, but the machine itself ran with unfailing determinism. This was the age of determinism, where freedom seemed an illusion, and mystery was steadily exiled from the universe. Human beings themselves were re–imagined as complex mechanisms, animated by predictable laws of matter. The soul – if it existed at all – was increasingly pressed to the margins.

Yet Newton himself resisted the full mechanistic interpretation. A deeply religious man, he studied biblical prophecy as much as physics. To him, the laws of motion and gravity revealed God's design, but they did not eliminate the divine. He worried that without divine correction, the solar system might collapse under instabilities. Thus, while posterity saw him as the prophet of mechanistic determinism, Newton himself kept one foot in the world of providence and faith.

The mechanistic universe carried profound implications for human self–understanding:

If the cosmos is a machine, is the human body also a machine?

If physical laws govern all motion, what becomes of freedom, morality, or soul?

If God is relegated to the role of watchmaker, winding the universe and stepping back, does prayer or ritual hold meaning?

These questions sparked centuries of debate, influencing Enlightenment thinkers, political philosophers, and even theologians. The success of Newtonian mechanics emboldened materialists, while alarming spiritualists.

After Newton, physics expanded into new domains, consolidating into what we now call the classical worldview. Its principles were elegant, universal, and deterministic.

The law of conservation of energy declared that energy can neither be created nor destroyed, only transformed. From steam engines to planetary motion, this principle held: nothing is lost, only converted.

The laws of thermodynamics, developed in the 19th century, refined this vision. The first law formalised energy conservation; the second law introduced the notion of entropy, the tendency of systems to move from order to disorder. Entropy explained why heat flows from hot to cold, why perpetual motion machines are impossible, and why time has a "direction." Together, these laws created a cosmos that appeared as a vast, rational machine. If one knew the position and velocity of every particle, then – in principle – one could calculate the entire future and reconstruct the entire past.

This radical confidence found its most striking expression in Laplace's demon:

"*An intelligence which could comprehend all the forces by which nature is animated … could embrace in a single formula the movements of the greatest bodies of the universe and those of the lightest atom. For such an intelligence nothing would be uncertain, and the future, as well as the past, would be present to its eyes.*"

In this universe, mystery seemed banished. Everything unfolded according to cause and effect, with no room for spontaneity, indeterminacy, or free will.

Newton identified only one universal force: gravity. Yet in the centuries that followed, others began to emerge. Electricity, once little more than sparks from rubbed amber, revealed its kinship with magnetism. Michael Faraday and James Clerk Maxwell showed that light itself was an electromagnetic wave, travelling at finite speed through the ether. Suddenly, the cosmos appeared not only mechanical but threaded with invisible fields of energy.

By the 19th century, scientists recognised four fundamental forces at work in the universe:

Gravity, holding planets and galaxies together.

Electromagnetism, governing light, electricity, and magnetism.

The strong nuclear force, binding protons and neutrons in the atom's core.

The weak nuclear force, enabling radioactive decay and fuelling the sun.

Together, these forces are described in the Standard Model of particle physics, where matter is composed of quarks and leptons, and forces are carried by bosons (photons, gluons, W and Z bosons). Gravity remains outside the Standard Model, awaiting unification.

This reductionist triumph – explaining the diversity of the universe through four forces and a handful of particles – seemed to vindicate the dream of total knowledge. And yet, the closer physics came to the "final theory," the more it revealed paradoxes and limits.

By the late 19th century, cracks were already visible in the edifice of classical physics. Certain phenomena simply could not be explained:

For instance, the blackbody radiation problem. Classical theory predicted that hot objects should radiate infinite energy at short wavelengths (the "ultraviolet catastrophe"). In 1900, Max Planck resolved this paradox by introducing the radical idea of energy quanta. In 1905, Albert Einstein built on this insight to explain the photoelectric effect: light striking a metal surface ejects electrons only if the light is above a certain frequency. If light were purely a wave, increasing intensity should suffice – but experiments showed it did not. Einstein argued that light behaved as particles (photons) carrying quanta of energy.

Soon, Niels Bohr extended quantum principles to the atom, proposing that electrons occupy discrete energy levels. Transitions between levels released or absorbed quanta of light, explaining atomic spectra that had baffled scientists.

Thus, within a few years, the universe was no longer governed by the smooth, deterministic laws of Newton. It was granular, probabilistic, and strange.

The photoelectric effect – classical wave theory of light could not explain why electrons were ejected from metals only above a certain threshold frequency. In 1905, Einstein explained it by treating light as quanta of energy (later called photons).

The orbit of Mercury – its slow precession around the Sun defied Newtonian mechanics, until Einstein's relativity offered a solution.

Each anomaly was a clue that the classical framework, for all its triumphs, was incomplete.

These were not poetic metaphors but measurable realities, embedded in the fabric of existence. Yet even as science mapped their mathematical precision, deeper mysteries arose. What was gravity, beyond a formula? How could "action at a distance" be possible? What was the ether through which electromagnetic waves travelled?

Every answer seemed to unlock new paradoxes, as if nature, while allowing glimpses of its order, always withheld its final secret.

The story of classical physics is not merely one of equations and experiments. It is the unfolding of a worldview: from Aristotle's teleological cosmos to Descartes' mechanistic machine, to Newton's universal laws, to Einstein's dynamic space–time. Each stage enlarged human understanding, yet each also revealed new puzzles.

By the early 20th century, Einstein's relativity and quantum mechanics would dethrone the clockwork model, replacing certainty with relativity, probability, and paradox. But even as these revolutions unfolded, Newton's synthesis remained the bedrock – the first true scientific unification of heaven and earth.

In his Annus Mirabilis (miracle year) of 1905, Albert Einstein published four papers, the most famous being on the Special Theory of Relativity.

Constancy of the speed of light: No matter how fast you move, light always travels at 299,792,458 m/s in a vacuum.

Relativity of simultaneity: Two events that seem simultaneous to one observer may not be simultaneous to another moving at a different speed.

Time dilation: Moving clocks tick more slowly relative to stationary ones.

Length contraction: Objects shorten in the direction of motion at high speeds.

This shattered Newton's absolutes. Space and time were no longer universal backdrops but relative and intertwined – a new fabric called spacetime.

Ten years later, Einstein advanced the General Theory of Relativity, a radical reimagining of gravity.

Gravity was not a force transmitted across space but the curvature of spacetime caused by mass and energy.

Planets orbit the sun not because they are "pulled" but because spacetime is curved by the sun's immense mass. Time itself bends in the presence of gravity: near a massive object, clocks tick more slowly.

This theory was spectacularly confirmed in 1919 when Arthur Eddington observed starlight bending around the sun during a solar eclipse. Suddenly, Einstein was a global icon.

Einstein's relativity profoundly unsettled old certainties:

There is no universal present; each observer carries their own slice of time. The distinction between past, present, and future as only a "stubbornly persistent illusion."

The Newtonian dream of prediction collapsed – the cosmos was not a rigid machine but a dynamic, shifting field.

In this sense, relativity reintroduced a kind of mystery into physics. The universe was not static, predictable clockwork but a malleable, interconnected web.

Werner Heisenberg's uncertainty principle (1927) showed that one could not simultaneously know both the position and momentum of a particle with arbitrary precision. Reality at its core was not deterministic but probabilistic. Particles did not have definite properties until measured; they existed as wavefunctions – clouds of probabilities.

This indeterminacy was not just a matter of human ignorance. It was baked into the structure of nature. The act of observation itself "collapsed" the wavefunction, forcing a single outcome from many possibilities. In this sense, the universe was no longer a perfectly predictable machine but a tapestry of probabilities and potentialities.

The contrast could not be more striking:

Classical science promised order, certainty, and predictability – a universe governed like a grand machine. Quantum science revealed ambiguity, mystery, and an irreducible role of the observer in shaping outcomes.

Einstein resisted this, arguing that quantum mechanics must be incomplete. Bohr countered that quantum uncertainty was the ultimate truth. Their debates – famously at the Solvay Conferences – continue to echo in philosophy, as we still wrestle with what quantum theory tells us about reality.

For the first time in centuries, science was not offering closure but opening doors. Consciousness, observation, and the act of measurement – previously dismissed as subjective – became central issues in the interpretation of physics itself.

Physics today rests on two great pillars:

Einstein's General Relativity (1915) – describing gravity as the curvature of spacetime, working flawlessly for stars, black holes, and galaxies.

Quantum Mechanics & Quantum Field Theory (1920s–1970s) – describing particles, forces, and probabilities at the subatomic scale, astonishingly successful in predicting experimental results.

Yet these two theories do not fit together. Relativity is smooth and continuous; quantum mechanics is discrete and probabilistic. Attempts to merge them – especially in extreme environments like black holes or the Big Bang – break down. This is sometimes called the "great incompatibility" at the heart of modern physics.

Perhaps this is why modern physics continues to search for a deeper theory - something that might unite the smooth geometry of relativity with the strange uncertainties of quantum mechanics. String theory, loop quantum gravity, and other proposals are attempts to glimpse a more fundamental order beneath the fractured surface of our current understanding. Yet the closer physics moves toward the beginning of the universe, the more its language begins to resemble something almost metaphysical. Space and time dissolve; matter becomes vibration, probability, or field; and the question quietly shifts from "What is the universe made of?" to "Why is there anything at all?"

As physics presses closer to this enquiry, it finds itself entering a strange territory. The equations can describe the expansion of the universe back to a tiny fraction of a second after its birth, but beyond that point they fall silent. At the edge of the Big Bang, the familiar categories of before and after, here and there, cause and effect begin to lose their meaning. We are no longer merely asking how stars and galaxies formed, but how existence itself emerged from whatever preceded - or perhaps underlies - the universe. It is at this threshold that the conversation naturally turns toward creation: not only the scientific question of origins, but the deeper human question of why there is something rather than nothing.

Long before science, human beings responded to this same mystery in a different way. Unable to express it through equations, they expressed it through myth, symbol, and story.

For ancient peoples, the night sky was not an abstract puzzle but a living canvas. The stars were woven into stories that explained origins, morality, and the structure of the world. In Aboriginal Australian Dreamtime, the stars mapped ancestral journeys; in Mesopotamia, they signalled the will of gods; in Greek tradition, they were heroes and monsters immortalised in constellations.

This human impulse reflects a profound psychological need: when faced with overwhelming mystery, we create narratives of belonging. Myths of origin allowed societies to anchor themselves in a cosmos that might otherwise feel indifferent or hostile.

It is striking that, though cultures were separated by oceans and centuries, many of their cosmogonies describe a transition from undifferentiated chaos to order. This pattern – of formlessness yielding to form reminds us of the discussion we had in the earlier parts where the act of observation collapses a field of probabilities into a definite state.

While myth and religion sought meaning through symbols and narratives, modern science offers its own grand story of origins: the cosmological model of the Big Bang.

According to current theory, the universe began around 13.8 billion years ago as an unimaginably hot, dense point – a singularity. In the first fraction of a second, space–time itself expanded rapidly in what is called cosmic inflation, smoothing the universe and seeding the distribution of galaxies.

Evidence for this story is both elegant and compelling:

The cosmic microwave background radiation – the faint afterglow of the primordial fireball – discovered in 1965 by Penzias and Wilson, now measured in exquisite detail by satellites like COBE, WMAP, and Planck.

The observed redshift of galaxies – discovered by Hubble – showing that space itself is stretching, carrying galaxies apart like raisins in rising dough.

The abundance of light elements (hydrogen, helium, lithium), which matches predictions of early nucleosynthesis.

Yet even the Big Bang story cannot fully answer the oldest question: Why is there something rather than nothing? Physics describes what happened after the first fraction of a second, but the origin of the singularity remains unknown. How could such vastness come to be?

This is not merely a scientific question. Since humanity first gazed at the night sky, cultures across the globe have woven myths, hymns, and philosophies to make sense of creation.

Among them, the Nasadiya Sukta of the Rig Veda (10.129) stands out as a hymn of astonishing depth and humility.

Verse 1

na āsat āsīn no sad āsīt tadānīṃ,

nāsīd rajo no vyomā paro yat |

kim āvarīvaḥ? kuha? kasya śarmann?

ambhaḥ kim āsīd gahanaṃ gabhīram ||

There was neither non–being nor being then;
There was no realm of air, no sky beyond it.
What covered it, and where? In whose protection?
What was the deep, unfathomable water?

Verse 2

na mṛtyur āsīd amṛtaṃ na tarhi,

na rātryā ahna āsīt praketāḥ |

ānīd avātaṃ svadhayā tad ekaṃ,

tasmād dhānyan na paraḥ kiṃ canāsa | |

There was no death, nor immortality then;
No sign of night or day was to be seen.
The One breathed, windless, by its own impulse;
Apart from it, nothing existed.

Verse 3

tama āsīt tamasā ghūḷam aghre,

apraketaṃ salilaṃ sarvam ā idam |

tucchyenābhv apihitaṃ yad āsīt,
tapasas tan mahinājāyataikam | |

Darkness was hidden in darkness,
All this was water without distinction.
That which, becoming, was covered by emptiness–
The great power of heat (tapas) was born.

Verse 4
kāmas tad agre sam avartatādhi,

manaso retaḥ prathamaṃ yad āsīt |
sato bandhūm asati nir avindan,

hṛdi pratīṣyā kavayo manīṣā | |

Desire (kāma) came upon that in the beginning–
That was the first seed of mind.
The sages, searching in their hearts,
Found the bond of being in non–being.

Verse 5

tirascīno vitato raśmir eṣām,

adhaḥ svid āsīd upari svid āsīt |
retodhā āsan mahimāna āsan,

svadhā avastāt prayatiḥ parastāt | |

Their cord was extended across–
Was there below? Was there above?
There were seed–bearers, there were powers;
There was self–impulse below, giving forth above.

Verse 6
ko addhā veda? ka iha pravocat,
kuta ājātā? kuta iyaṃ visṛṣṭiḥ? |
arvāg devā asya visarjanenā,
atho ko veda yata ābabhūva | |

Who really knows? Who can here proclaim
Whence it arose, whence this creation?
The gods are later than this world's becoming–
Who then knows whence it has come?

Verse 7
iyaṃ visṛṣṭir yata ābabhūva,
yadi vā dadhe yadi vā na |
yo asyādhyakṣaḥ parame vyoman,
so aṅga veda yadi vā na veda | |

Whence this creation has arisen–
Perhaps it formed itself, or perhaps it did not–
He, the overseer in the highest heaven,
He alone knows, or perhaps He does not know.

This hymn is extraordinary not only for its beauty but for its epistemic humility. Unlike the commanding certainties of other traditions, here the poet embraces unknown: even the overseer of heaven may not know. The progression–darkness, water, desire, mind, order, question–is as close to a philosophical cosmology as ancient humanity dared.

Here, creation is framed as a mystery beyond even the gods, suggesting that existence itself resists final explanation. This humility stands in contrast to traditions that assert dogmatic origins and resonates with modern cosmology's admission that while we model the Big Bang, we cannot say what (if anything) preceded it.

The Sukta foreshadows the Buddhist notion of emptiness (śūnyatā) and the later quantum recognition that at fundamental levels, reality is indeterminate. The Sukta remains unique for its radical humility. In a world where myths often serve power and dogma, this hymn teaches a different lesson: that the greatest wisdom lies not in knowing, but in reverence before the unknown.

If the Nasadiya Sukta is marked by its piercing questions and humility, other traditions approach the question of origins with more confidence – yet often describe remarkably similar transitions from nothingness or chaos to cosmos.

In Hesiod's Theogony, the beginning is Chaos. From Chaos came Gaia (Earth), Tartarus (the Abyss), and Eros (Desire). Creation unfolds as a genealogy: gods begetting gods, order emerging from struggle. The Greek narrative does not speak of a single principle but of multiplicity, conflict, and drama. The cosmos is not born of mystery or singular command but from the interplay of primordial beings. It reflects a worldview where divine forces mirror human passions–strife, love, ambition.

In Norse mythology, creation begins in Ginnungagap, a yawning chasm between two primal realms – Muspelheim (fire) and Niflheim (ice). Where they met, steam and sparks formed the first giant, Ymir, from whose body the gods fashioned the world. Again, existence emerges not from order but from elemental tension.

The Hebrew Genesis narrative is more linear and declarative: "In the beginning, God created the heavens and the earth. The earth was formless and void, and darkness was over the deep" (Genesis 1:1–2). Unlike the Vedic hymn, there is no uncertainty. Time, space, and beings exist because God wills it so. This narrative emphasises divine sovereignty and human subordination to a creator. For millennia, this framework shaped Western theological thought: creation as purposeful act by a transcendent deity.

In the Bible, creation begins not with humanity but with the universe itself. "In the beginning, God created the heavens and the earth." Before there was light, matter, time, or life, there was only God and the formless void. The earth was "without form and void," and darkness covered the deep, until creation unfolded through a series of divine utterances: "Let there be light." In this vision, existence is not self-arising but willed into being by a transcendent source that stands outside the universe and precedes it. Humanity appears only near the end of the process, as part of a much larger cosmic unfolding.

There are also later biblical passages that make this even more metaphysical. The Gospel of John opens with:

"*In the beginning was the Word... All things were made through him.*"

Here, the universe emerges through the "Word" - the Greek Logos - suggesting an underlying principle, intelligence, or ordering structure behind creation. This can be interesting to juxtapose with the Dao, Brahman, or even the modern scientific search for a unifying law beneath reality. The Bible therefore moves beyond the origin of humanity and asks the larger question of how existence itself arose from something prior, timeless, and unseen.

In the Dao De Jing, Laozi describes the Dao as prior to heaven and earth: "*There was something undifferentiated and complete, before heaven and earth were born. Silent, formless, it stands alone and does not change. It is the mother of the world.*"

Unlike the Hebrew God or Greek gods, the Dao is impersonal, ineffable, and beyond categories. It is not a being but the way things are. Creation is not an event but a spontaneous unfolding of the Dao into the "ten thousand things."

This resonates strongly with the Nasadiya Sukta's refusal to personify creation. Both traditions accept mystery and emphasise the limits of language.

The Qur'an describes creation with vivid imagery: "*Do not those who disbelieve see that the heavens and the earth were joined together, then We split them apart?*" (21:30). This recalls the Big Bang metaphor, where unity becomes multiplicity.

Islamic thought emphasises *tawhid* – the oneness of God. Unlike the questioning tone of the Vedic seer, the Qur'an asserts certainty: God knows, God wills, God creates. Yet mystics such as Rumi later interpret creation as an unfolding of divine love: "*The universe was brought into being so that it might know love.*"

Mesoamerican Narratives define creation through trial and error. In the Mayan Popol Vuh, the gods attempt creation multiple times. First, humans are formed from mud, but they crumble. Then from wood, but they lack souls. Finally, from maize–the sacred crop–they succeed.

Here creation is experimental, marked by failure and learning. It reflects a worldview where human identity is bound to agriculture and community. Unlike the transcendent certainties of Genesis, the Mayan gods struggle, err, and adjust.

Meanwhile, Australian Aboriginal Dreaming stories describe a timeless realm where ancestral beings sang the land, rivers, animals, and people into existence. Creation is not a singular event but a songline – an ongoing process that links landscape, memory, and identity. Though diverse, these narratives share recurring motifs:

A primordial nothingness or chaos.
A principle of emergence (desire, word, sound, divine act).
A transition to order, form, and differentiation.

The striking similarity suggests that human imagination, across cultures, converges on archetypal patterns when faced with the beginning enigma.

Here, science converges with the humility of the Nasadiya Sukta. Cosmologists such as Stephen Hawking suggested that the question "What came before the Big Bang?" may be meaningless, as time itself may have begun with the universe.

Standing in this vastness, whether through mythic imagination or scientific cosmology, we return inevitably to the human predicament. Why does consciousness exist in such a universe?

If the cosmos is so immense, why should one fragile planet host reflective beings capable of asking why it exists at all? This paradox – the smallness of humanity and the depth of human awareness – will guide the rest of our exploration.

Perhaps the true mystery is not the Big Bang, but the fact that from stardust has emerged a mind that can contemplate stardust. This is where cosmology, physics, and philosophy converge. And this is where the problem of self and continuity will find its larger stage: in a universe vast beyond measure, the illusion of self and the mystery of consciousness demand explanation.

The Big Bang theory speaks of an origin 13.8 billion years ago but cannot describe "before." Quantum cosmology speculates about fluctuations, multiverses, or eternal inflation. Yet the ultimate "why" remains unanswered.

Here science unexpectedly converges with the Nasadiya Sukta. Both recognise limits. Both say: there is a boundary beyond which knowledge falters. Science does not yet know what preceded the Big Bang. The Vedic seer asks – perhaps no one knows.

What emerges from this tapestry is not a single truth but a spectrum of human attempts to understand the origin. Some claim certainty, some embrace doubt. Some see a God, some see chaos, some see an ineffable principle.

Interestingly, Einstein himself resisted connecting physics with consciousness. He often dismissed quantum mechanics' probabilistic interpretation as incomplete ("*God does not play dice*"). He sought hidden variables that would restore order. And yet, his own words – acknowledging the illusory nature of time, the unity of the cosmos, and the relativity of reality – point to a recognition of something beyond the individual self.

He could not quite step into the realm that mystics, Vedantins, or Buddhists had long explored: that awareness itself may be the fundamental reality.

Relativity was not the final revolution. Even as Einstein rose to prominence, a younger generation – Bohr, Heisenberg, Schrödinger – unveiled the strange world of quantum mechanics. Here, determinism gave way to probability; particles behaved as both waves and quanta; observation itself seemed to collapse possibilities into actualities.

Einstein never accepted quantum indeterminacy. With Podolsky and Rosen, he proposed the famous EPR paradox, suggesting "hidden variables" must exist to restore order. Bohr countered that quantum uncertainty was fundamental.

This debate echoed deeper divides: Einstein's longing for a rational, deterministic cosmos versus Bohr's acceptance of a probabilistic, observer–entangled reality. Einstein's discomfort showed his limits; he glimpsed the illusion of time but resisted the possibility that consciousness itself might shape reality.

The 20th century did not stop at the quantum. New radical theories emerged:

Quantum field theory (QFT): The universe is not made of particles but of fields; particles are excitations of underlying quantum fields.

String theory: Proposes that all particles are tiny vibrating strings in higher dimensions.

Multiverse hypotheses: Quantum mechanics may imply parallel universes where all possibilities are realised.

Each of these theories expands the sense of mystery: reality is no longer a simple, singular machine but an infinite play of possibilities, vibrations, and unseen dimensions.

Despite its successes, physics still skirts around the problem of consciousness. The quantum formalism works, but what collapses the wave function? Instruments? Mathematics? Or awareness itself?

Some physicists argue for decoherence – interaction with the environment.

Others, like Wigner, insist that mind is indispensable.

Mystics, Vedantins, Buddhists, and Sufis go further: consciousness is primary, matter secondary.

Where myths once spoke of chaos giving birth to order, physics spoke of forces shaping matter. Where religion once saw divine will, science saw natural law. Yet both myth and science ultimately encounter mystery: the question of origins, the meaning of time, and the nature of consciousness.

As we cross the threshold into quantum mechanics, the secure world of determinism will dissolve into a universe of probabilities, entanglements, and paradoxes. If classical physics gave us the confidence of Laplace's demon, quantum physics will humble us once more – echoing the agnostic spirit of the Nasadiya Sukta.

We have followed the story of the Big Bang and the birth of the cosmos not merely to understand how galaxies formed, but because hidden within these questions is something more intimate. In asking how the universe began, we are also asking how we came to be here to ask the question at all. What is this strange emergence of matter into life, of life into awareness, of awareness into the restless search for meaning? The deeper we look into the origin of the universe, the more the enquiry turns back upon ourselves. Perhaps the search for the beginning is, in the end, also a search for purpose - not a final answer handed down from outside, but an invitation to look more deeply into the mystery of existence itself.

Strangely, many of the great spiritual enquiries begin with the same questions. One of the most profound appears in the dialogue between Devi and Shiva in the Vigyan Bhairava Tantra about 5000 years ago, a text traditionally regarded as one of the oldest explorations of human consciousness, predating organised religion and many later yogic traditions. Devi asks him the same questions that still haunt philosophy and physics today: What is this universe? From where does it arise? What is the nature of the self, of awareness, of reality? We will return to this dialogue in later chapters, for it stands as a bridge between the outer search of science and the inner search of consciousness.

IN SEARCH OF A PURPOSE

There is a quiet question that lives in almost every human heart.

It does not always appear as words. Often it remains hidden beneath the routines of daily life, masked by responsibilities, ambitions, relationships, and distractions. Yet when the noise subsides – in moments of solitude, grief, wonder, or uncertainty – the question emerges with disarming simplicity:

Why do I exist?

Why this life, this body, this brief appearance in a universe that stretches across unimaginable scales of time and space?

The question is as old as humanity itself. From the earliest cave paintings to the most sophisticated scientific theories, human beings have searched for meaning in existence. Civilisations have risen and fallen, philosophies have been written and rewritten, religions have formed and transformed – yet the question persists.

In every culture we find some variation of the same enquiry:

What is the purpose of life?
Who am I?
What happens when life ends?
Is there something more behind the visible world?

The persistence of these questions reveals something fundamental about the human condition. Unlike other animals, humans possess the unusual capacity to reflect upon their own existence. We are not only participants in life; we are observers of it. We can step back, examine our experiences, and ask what it all means.

This capacity for self–reflection is both a gift and a burden. It allows us to create art, science, philosophy, and civilisation itself. But it also confronts us with the unsettling realisation that our lives are temporary and uncertain.

We are born without knowing why.
We live without fully understanding how.
And we die without certainty about what follows.

Faced with this existential uncertainty, humanity has naturally sought frameworks that can provide orientation and meaning.

For most of history, the primary framework has been religion.

Religious traditions emerged in every corner of the world, often independently yet remarkably similar in their underlying concerns. They offered narratives that explained where we came from, why we are here, and what ultimately happens after death.

Creation myths described the origins of the universe and humanity. Moral codes defined right and wrong behaviour. Rituals provided a sense of belonging and continuity with the past. Sacred texts offered guidance for navigating the complexities of life.

These traditions served vital social and psychological functions. They created communities bound by shared beliefs and values. They established ethical frameworks that helped societies maintain stability and cooperation. They provided comfort in the face of suffering and death.

Religion, in this sense, is not merely belief. It is a social system of cohesion and order – a structure through which cultures organise meaning, morality, and collective identity.

It answers questions such as:

How should we live together?
What is right and wrong?
What duties do we have toward one another?
What traditions should we preserve?

Through temples, churches, mosques, monasteries, and rituals, religion gives form to these shared values.

But alongside these outward structures, there has always existed another kind of enquiry – quieter, more personal, and often more radical.

This enquiry does not ask merely how to live within society. It asks something more fundamental:

What is the nature of the self who is living this life?

Religion and spirituality have often offered different kinds of answers to this question. Religion may respond through stories, doctrines, and teachings: the self is a soul created by God, an individual being journeying through the world, accountable to a higher order. Spiritual enquiry, by contrast, often suspends inherited answers and asks the question directly. Rather than beginning with what one is told to believe, it asks: when all roles, memories, thoughts, and identities fall silent, what remains?

This shift in emphasis marks one way of distinguishing religion from spirituality. Though the two often overlap, they are not always the same. Religion usually provides an outer framework: traditions, rituals, stories, ethics, and communities through which people relate to the sacred. Yet within many religions there have also been inward paths - contemplative, mystical, and experiential. Spiritual enquiry places its centre of gravity there. It turns inward, asking not simply what one should believe, but what can be directly discovered about the nature of experience, consciousness, and reality.

Religion asks:

What should we believe?
How should we worship?
What practices connect us with the sacred?

Spiritual enquiry asks:

Who is the one who believes?
Who is the one who worships?
What is the nature of the self who seeks the sacred?

These two movements are not necessarily in conflict. Many religious traditions contain profound spiritual teachings within them. The mystics of Christianity, the sages of Vedanta, the Zen masters of Buddhism, the Sufi poets of Islam, and the contemplatives of many other traditions all turned their attention inward, asking not merely how to serve God but how to understand the nature of consciousness itself.

Yet history shows that institutional religion and inner enquiry do not always coexist comfortably.

Institutions require stability. They preserve doctrines and practices that provide continuity across generations. Spiritual enquiry, by contrast, often challenges assumptions that institutions take for granted.

A person devoted to a religious tradition may seek comfort, guidance, and belonging within that tradition.

A seeker engaged in spiritual enquiry may instead ask unsettling questions:

Is the self I take myself to be real?
What remains if identity dissolves?
Is consciousness something personal, or something more fundamental?

These questions do not reject religion. Rather, they move beyond the boundaries of belief and into direct investigation.

Across cultures and centuries – from the Vedic and Buddhist traditions to the Norse, Greek, Biblical, and Islamic worlds – there are persistent accounts of encounters between human beings and what were understood to be divine or otherworldly intelligences. Whether interpreted literally, symbolically, or psychologically, these accounts share a striking consistency: they tend to occur under conditions that profoundly alter ordinary consciousness. Sages meditating for years in solitude. Prophets fasting in deserts or on mountains. Mystics withdrawing into states of deep contemplation or prayer.

If we look carefully at the circumstances under which many of the ancient encounters were said to occur, an interesting pattern begins to emerge.

Across cultures, moments of interaction with divine or unseen beings often took place under conditions that profoundly altered ordinary consciousness. Sages meditated for years in solitude. Prophets fasted in deserts or mountains. Mystics withdrew from society and entered states of deep contemplation or prayer.

The Buddha himself attained enlightenment after prolonged meditation and ascetic practice beneath the Bodhi tree. Moses is said to have encountered the divine on Mount Sinai after periods of retreat and spiritual preparation. Muhammad received the first revelations while meditating in the cave of Hira. Many Hindu sages described visions of devas while engaged in intense tapas.

In Norse mythology, Odin gained wisdom after hanging from the world tree for nine nights in a state of sacrifice and altered awareness. Greek oracles entered trance–like states before delivering messages believed to come from Apollo.

Although the cultural interpretations differ, the psychological conditions share remarkable similarities. Modern neuroscience has begun to explore what happens to the brain under such circumstances.

Practices such as meditation, fasting, sensory deprivation, rhythmic chanting, and prolonged solitude can profoundly change patterns of neural activity. Studies using brain imaging have shown that these practices can reduce activity in networks responsible for maintaining the ordinary narrative sense of self – particularly regions associated with what neuroscientists call the default mode network.

When this network quiets, the usual boundaries between self and world can become less rigid. Individuals may report experiences of unity, expanded awareness, or the sense of encountering presences beyond the ordinary sense of identity. In deep contemplative states, the brain may also shift into patterns dominated by slow rhythmic oscillations or highly synchronised activity across distant neural regions. Such states are often associated with feelings of clarity, insight, and profound meaning.

None of this proves that encounters with other realms literally occurred. Yet it does suggest that the human brain is capable of entering states of perception very different from those that dominate everyday life.

Under such conditions, the mind may interpret unusual sensory or cognitive experiences using the symbolic language available within its culture. In one civilisation the experience might be described as the appearance of an angel; in another, a deva; in another, a god or spirit.

From the perspective of neuroscience, these interpretations could represent the brain's effort to organise extraordinary experiences into familiar forms.

Yet another possibility remains open.

If consciousness itself is more fundamental than the individual brain – as some philosophers and physicists have speculated – then altered states of awareness might allow the mind to access aspects of reality normally filtered out by ordinary perception.

Modern science reminds us how limited our sensory window truly is. Human eyes detect only a tiny portion of the electromagnetic spectrum. Our ears hear only a narrow band of vibrations. Even our perception of time and space is shaped by the architecture of our nervous system.

It is therefore conceivable that reality contains layers of complexity that our ordinary senses rarely register.

In recent decades, neuroscience has begun to explore a provocative idea about how perception itself works. According to a theory often called predictive processing, the brain does not simply receive information from the world and interpret it. Instead, it actively constructs a model of reality and continually updates that model using incoming sensory data.

In this view, perception is not a passive recording of the world but a dynamic negotiation between expectation and observation.

The brain constantly generates predictions about what it expects to encounter: shapes, sounds, movements, patterns of behaviour. Incoming sensory signals are then compared against these predictions. When the signals match the brain's expectations, experience feels stable and coherent. When they do not match, the brain revises its internal model.

What we experience as "reality," therefore, may be partly shaped by the predictions the brain has learned to make.

This insight has far–reaching implications.

It suggests that our perception of the world is not a direct window into reality, but an interpretive construction shaped by memory, culture, language, and prior experience.

Different societies, operating with different symbolic frameworks, might therefore interpret unusual experiences in very different ways.

An unexpected perception in an ancient society steeped in religious cosmology might be interpreted as the appearance of a god, an angel, or a celestial messenger. The same experience in a modern context might be interpreted psychologically, neurologically, or dismissed as coincidence.

Predictive processing does not claim that spiritual experiences are illusions. Rather, it proposes that the human brain plays an active role in shaping how such experiences are perceived and understood.

If consciousness encounters something unfamiliar – whether internal or external – the mind may interpret it using the symbolic language available to it.

This possibility may help explain why encounters with divine or unseen beings appear in so many ancient traditions, each framed within the imagery and cosmology of its culture.

Yet the deeper mystery remains unresolved.

For even if the brain constructs models of reality, the question persists:
What is the deeper reality that those models attempt to represent?

The predictive brain may shape the theatre of experience, but it does not necessarily explain the stage upon which that theatre unfolds.

Ancient traditions may have attempted to describe such possibilities using the language available to them – gods, angels, devas, or spirits.

Whether these encounters were psychological, symbolic, or glimpses into dimensions of reality not yet understood remains an open question. What is clear, however, is that human consciousness possesses a remarkable capacity to move beyond its ordinary boundaries. And when it does, the experience often carries the sense that the universe is far more alive, mysterious, and interconnected than the everyday mind assumes. But their presence across cultures reveals something important about the human search for meaning.

For millennia, human beings have sensed that existence may extend beyond the visible world. They have felt that consciousness itself might connect us to a deeper order of reality.

The question, therefore, is not merely whether such encounters occurred.

The deeper question is this:

What kind of universe would make them possible? And what might that imply about the nature of the consciousness through which we experience it?

One final question naturally arises from this long history of encounters between humans and the unseen.

For much of ancient history, stories of interactions with gods, angels, devas, or other beings appear frequently in cultural memory. Sacred texts, myths, and traditions describe moments when the human world seemed to intersect with other realms.

Yet in the recorded history of the last two or three millennia, such encounters appear to have grown increasingly rare – at least in ways that shape entire civilisation.

Why might this be so?

One possibility is that human societies have gradually changed the way they interpret extraordinary experiences. As scientific frameworks developed, events that once would have been understood in spiritual or mythological terms began to be explained through natural processes.

Another possibility is that the conditions under which such encounters occurred have become less common. Ancient sages often spent years in solitude, fasting, meditating, or withdrawing from ordinary social life. These practices profoundly altered consciousness, perhaps opening perceptual states rarely encountered in the rhythms of modern life.

It is also possible that such interactions never disappeared at all, but that the language and forms through which they are expressed have simply changed. What earlier cultures described as gods or angels might today be interpreted through different conceptual frameworks.

Or perhaps the truth lies somewhere between these possibilities.

The Buddha said, his teachings are like a raft used to cross a river. Once the crossing is complete, one does not carry the raft on one's back. Even the teachings themselves must eventually be released.

The implication is subtle but profound: the mind that clings – even to ideas about truth – remains entangled.

Mystical traditions across cultures often reached comparable conclusions.

The Sufi poet Rumi wrote,

"We are the mirror and the face in it."

In this poetic language, the apparent separation between observer and observed begins to dissolve. Ibn Arabi, another influential Sufi thinker, described the universe as the self–disclosure of a single reality expressing itself through countless forms.

These mystical intuitions sometimes find surprising echoes in modern science.

The Big Bang theory suggests that space and time themselves emerged from an early state of extraordinary density and energy. From that beginning, the universe expanded, cooled, and eventually produced stars, planets, and living organisms.

Relativity reshaped our understanding of time and space, showing that they are not absolute frameworks but interwoven aspects of a dynamic spacetime influenced by motion and gravity.

Quantum mechanics went further still, revealing a world where particles behave as waves, where multiple possibilities can coexist in superposition, and where entangled systems remain correlated across vast distances. Within this vastness, the appearance of conscious beings introduces something remarkable.

Without awareness, galaxies would continue their silent revolutions unnoticed. With awareness, even a fleeting human life becomes capable of reflecting on the cosmos itself.

William James, one of the founders of modern psychology, described consciousness as a "stream" – continuous, flowing, and dynamic rather than composed of fixed elements.

Gurdjieff later warned that many human beings live mechanically, caught in habitual patterns without ever awakening to deeper layers of awareness.

Meister Eckhart, centuries earlier, urged seekers to release images and concepts so that the divine could be experienced directly rather than imagined.

The universe may be far more complex than the narrow slice we ordinarily perceive. Modern science itself reminds us that most of the cosmos is composed of matter and energy we cannot directly observe.

Whether the ancient stories describe symbolic insights, altered states of consciousness, or encounters with aspects of reality not yet understood, they reflect a persistent human intuition: that existence may contain layers beyond the visible world.

Yet even if such possibilities exist, the great spiritual traditions repeatedly emphasise the same point.

The deepest transformation does not depend on encounters with other realms.

It begins with the quiet investigation of our own consciousness.

For the most mysterious phenomenon in the universe may not be the appearance of gods or angels, but the simple fact that awareness itself exists.

And yet, after all the stories, theories, religions, and philosophies, the original questions remain. What is the purpose of life? Who am I? Why is there something rather than nothing? We search for answers because something within us feels incomplete, as though there is a missing piece that, once found, would finally make sense of everything.

But perhaps there is another question, quieter and more unsettling than the rest. Who, exactly, is the one asking? We assume there is a solid "I" standing at the centre of experience - a thinker searching for truth, a self-moving through time, asking what it all means. Yet the deeper we look, the more uncertain this seeker begins to appear. Is it something real and enduring, or is it itself part of the mystery we are trying to solve?

Yet if we are honest, much of our searching is directed outward. We look for meaning in achievement, possessions, relationships, pleasures, distractions, beliefs, identities, and the countless small occupations of everyday life. We fill our days with movement and noise, hoping that somewhere among these things we will discover the answer we seek. But rarely do we pause and turn inward. Rarely do we ask whether the purpose we are searching for can be found in the world at all, or whether we have simply been looking in the wrong place.

The old Sufi stories tell of a man searching frantically beneath a streetlamp late at night.

He is on his hands and knees, moving anxiously through the dust, peering into every crack in the road. A passer-by stops to help and, after some time, asks, "What have you lost?" "My key," the man replies. Together they search for several more minutes, until the passer-by finally asks, "Where did you lose it?" The man points toward his dark house in the distance. "Inside." Bewildered, the passer-by asks, "Then why are you looking here?" The man answers, "Because there is more light outside."

Perhaps we do the same. We search for meaning where it is easiest to look - in the bright distractions of the outer world - while what we are really seeking lies in the quieter, darker place within. Jalal ad-Din Muhammad Rumi wrote: "*You wander from room to room hunting for the diamond necklace that is already around your neck.*"

Before we can understand the meaning of existence, we may first need to understand the one who seeks that meaning. And it is there, in the seemingly familiar sense of "I," that our enquiry must now turn.

And if we wish to understand that mystery, the journey ultimately turns inward.

THE ILLUSION OF THE ONE WHO SEEKS

We saw that the present is not universal. That matter is not solid substance but structured interaction. That colour does not exist in objects but emerges from electromagnetic interaction and neural processing. That what appears "continuous" is assembled from discrete physical events.

Now we turn inward.

To turn inward does not mean withdrawing from the world or becoming lost in abstraction. It means directing attention toward the one who is experiencing. We spend our lives watching objects, world, events, people, and problems, yet rarely do we watch the movement of our own mind. Thoughts arise, emotions surge, memories appear, desires and fears pull us in different directions - and almost immediately we become entangled in them, taking them to be "me" and "mine." To turn inward is to pause and observe. To notice thoughts without being carried away by them. To watch feelings arise and pass. To ask, quietly and honestly: who is aware of all this?

There is an old story of a fish who spent its life searching for the ocean. It swam from reef to reef, from current to current, asking every creature it met where the ocean could be found. At last, exhausted, it asked an older fish. The old fish smiled and said, "You are in it." "No," replied the young fish, "this is only water. I am looking for the ocean." In the same way, we often search outside ourselves for what can only be discovered by becoming aware of the very consciousness in which our thoughts, emotions, and experience already appear.

If the external world is not as it appears, what of the experience of that world?

Is perception a passive reception of reality?
Or is it an active construction?

For centuries, common sense suggested that perception is straightforward. The world exists independently. Light enters the eyes. Sounds enter the ears. Information travels inward. The brain registers what is already there.

Reality is simply received. But neuroscience suggests something more subtle.

Perception is not passive reception. It is active inference.

The Brain Does Not See Light – It Interprets Signals.

When photons strike the retina, they do not produce images. They trigger chemical changes in photoreceptor cells. These changes alter electrical potential. Signals propagate along the optic nerve. They reach the visual cortex, where patterns of neural firing are interpreted.

At no stage does a tiny image appear inside the head.

There is no internal screen.

Consider something seemingly simple: standing in front of a mirror and seeing your own reflection.

It feels immediate. Effortless. As though a person inside the body is looking outward through the eyes at another person – oneself – in the glass.

But what actually happens?

Light from the surrounding environment strikes the surface of the body. Photons reflect off the skin, the hair, the eyes. These reflected photons travel through space and strike the mirror. The mirror does not "create" an image. Its surface simply reflects incoming light according to the law of reflection – angle in equals angle out. The photons bounce off the mirror and travel back toward the eyes.

Only now does the biological process begin.

Photons enter the eye through the cornea, pass through the pupil, and are focused by the lens onto the retina at the back of the eye. The retina is not a screen showing a picture. It is living neural tissue. Photoreceptor cells – rods and cones – absorb photons and convert light energy into electrochemical signals.

Each receptor responds only to local changes in light intensity or wavelength. No receptor sees a face. No receptor recognises a self. Each detects tiny variations in brightness and colour.

These signals are transmitted through layers of retinal neurons, compressed, processed, and sent through the optic nerve toward the brain. Along the way, information is already being filtered. Edges are enhanced. Contrast is amplified. Redundant signals are suppressed.

By the time the signals reach the visual cortex at the back of the brain, they are no longer raw light. They are patterns of electrical activity distributed across networks of neurons.

The brain reconstructs depth using binocular disparity – the slight difference between the two eyes. It reconstructs shape from contrast gradients. It assigns colour by comparing activity among different cone receptors. It stabilises the image despite constant micro–movements of the eyes.

The image in the mirror is not located inside the skull.

Nor is it located in the glass.

It is an active neural construction – a model generated by coordinated brain activity.

Now consider something subtler.

The image formed on the retina is inverted – upside down and reversed. There is no tiny person inside the brain flipping it upright. Instead, through development and experience, neural circuits learn to interpret spatial relations consistently.

Even recognition of the face in the mirror is not immediate. Infants do not automatically recognise themselves in front of a mirror. Self–recognition develops over time as the brain learns to associate certain visual patterns with bodily sensations, movement, and memory.

When you move your hand in front of the mirror and see the reflected hand move, the brain correlates visual input with motor signals. It predicts the movement before it happens. When prediction and perception align, the image is experienced as "mine."

The sense that the reflected person is "me" is not given by the mirror. It is constructed by neural integration of visual data, proprioceptive signals, memory, and expectation.

At no stage is there a central observer watching a screen.

There is no theatre inside the head.

There is only distributed processing, giving rise to a unified experience.

And yet, standing in front of the mirror, it feels as though a solid self is looking at a solid world. And "me".

The earlier questions now return.

If matter is structured interaction, and if perception is constructed from neural processing, then the reflection in the mirror is not a direct encounter with reality. It is the brain's best predictive model of light patterns correlated with a body.

From an evolutionary perspective, the nervous system did not emerge to reveal ultimate truth. It emerged to ensure survival. Organisms that could distinguish self from environment had an advantage. Boundaries matter in biology. Skin separates interior from exterior. Pain signals threat. Hunger signals need. The primitive roots of "self" are embedded in bodily regulation long before language appears.

The human brain is not an abstract seat of consciousness. It is a biological structure weighing roughly 1.3 to 1.5 kilograms, composed primarily of water, lipids, proteins, and salts. It contains approximately eighty–six billion neurons, along with an even greater number of glial cells that support and regulate neural activity.

At first glance, it is simply tissue.

And yet from this tissue arises memory, perception, emotion, and the sense of self.

To understand how this happens, one must look at the neuron.

Neurons are a specialised cell designed for communication. Each neuron has a cell body, branching dendrites that receive signals, and a long projection called an axon that transmits signals to other neurons. But neurons do not communicate by mechanical movement. They communicate through electrochemical processes.

The "electricity" of the brain is not electricity in the sense of wires plugged into a socket. It is generated by the controlled movement of charged ions – primarily sodium, potassium, calcium, and chloride – across the neuron's membrane.

Every neuron maintains a voltage difference between its interior and exterior. This resting membrane potential exists because ion channels and pumps regulate the distribution of charged particles across the cell membrane. The most important of these is the sodium–potassium pump, which actively transports sodium ions out of the cell and potassium ions into it, creating an electrical gradient.

When a neuron receives sufficient input from other neurons, ion channels open. Sodium ions rush inward. This rapid change in voltage creates what is known as an action potential – a brief electrical impulse that travels down the axon.

The action potential is not a continuous wave of electricity. It is a discrete, self–propagating electrochemical event.

When it reaches the end of the axon, the electrical signal triggers the release of chemical messengers called neurotransmitters into a tiny gap between neurons known as the synapse. These neurotransmitters bind to receptors on the next neuron, altering its electrical state and increasing or decreasing the likelihood that it will fire.

Through billions of such interactions occurring every second, patterns of neural activity emerge.

These patterns are not static. They are dynamic, constantly shifting networks of excitation and inhibition.

When light strikes the retina, photoreceptors convert photons into changes in membrane potential. These signals travel through retinal circuits to the optic nerve, then to the thalamus, and finally to the visual cortex. There, distributed populations of neurons process orientation, motion, colour, and depth.

When sound waves vibrate the eardrum, mechanical motion is converted into electrical signals within the cochlea. Hair cells translate vibration into neural impulses that travel to the auditory cortex.

When the skin encounters pressure or temperature change, specialised receptors convert mechanical or thermal energy into electrical activity transmitted through spinal pathways to the somatosensory cortex.

Taste involves chemical molecules binding to receptor cells on the tongue. Smell involves airborne molecules binding to receptors in the nasal cavity. In each case, the physical stimulus is transformed into patterns of neural firing.

The brain does not contain colours, sounds, or textures.
It contains electrical and chemical activity.

From this activity, experience arises.

There is no central control room where signals arrive to be watched.

Instead, perception emerges from coordinated activity across distributed neural networks.

The sensation of a red apple is not located in one place. Colour processing, shape recognition, memory association, and emotional response occur in different regions, yet are synchronised into a unified experience.

Unity arises from integration.

Electricity in the brain is therefore not mysterious. It is the movement of ions creating voltage changes across membranes. But the organisation of those electrical events – the patterns they form – gives rise to perception and behaviour.

The solidity of the chair, the greenness of the leaf, the sound of a voice – all are patterns of neural activity shaped by interaction with the environment.

The earlier destabilisation now deepens.
Matter is structured interaction.
Perception is constructed representation.
The brain is electrochemical process.

And yet, experience feels unified.
It feels centred.

It feels as though there is someone to whom all of this is happening.

That sense of centre remains to be examined.

Electric impulses travel. Neurotransmitters bind. Networks activate and inhibit one another. Sensory signals are integrated with memory and prediction. Out of this coordinated electrochemical activity, a coherent world appears.

At no point in this process does a separate observer enter the system.

There is no anatomical structure inside the brain that corresponds to a central witness. Neuroscience has mapped regions associated with vision, language, memory, emotion, decision–making. It has not found a seat of the self – no command centre where a homunculus sits, watching signals arrive.

What is found instead are processes influencing other processes.

Electrical activity gives rise to patterns.
Patterns integrate into representations.
Representations generate behaviour.

And yet, alongside this activity, there is the persistent sense: "I am here."

This sense feels singular, continuous, located behind the eyes.

But within the neural description, there is no identifiable entity that matches that feeling.

There are only dynamic interactions.

If matter is structured probability,
if perception is constructed representation,
if the brain is electrochemical process,

then what exactly is this "I" that claims ownership of experience?

The human brain is composed of roughly eighty–six billion neurons. Each neuron is a living cell specialised for electrical and chemical signalling. These cells communicate through electrochemical processes: ions move across membranes; neurotransmitters cross synapses; voltage changes propagate along axons.

At every stage, the underlying mechanism remains physical.

Ions are atoms.
Charges are electromagnetic phenomena.
Chemical gradients arise from molecular structure.

There is no foreign substance introduced.

From the perspective of physics and chemistry, nothing fundamentally new appears.
And yet, when organised in a particular way, this matter does something extraordinary:

It generates experience.

Right now, there is experience.

Not conceptually.
Directly.

There is seeing.
There is reading.
There is awareness of words forming meaning.

This fact – that there is something it is like to be you – is undeniable.

The philosopher William James described consciousness as a "stream," continuous and flowing. More recently, Thomas Nagel asked a simple but powerful question: What is it like to be a bat? His point was not about behaviour, but about subjective perspective. Even if we knew everything about the bat's neurobiology, we might still not know what it feels like from within.

This is the puzzle. But this is not yet a claim about consciousness being separate/distinct from matter.

Physics explains structure.
Chemistry explains bonding.
Biology explains organisation.

But none of these descriptions yet explain why there is experience at all.

The molecules in your brain obey quantum rules.
The electrons follow probability distributions.
The neurons exchange signals according to electrochemical laws.

At no identifiable point does physics announce:
"Experience begins here."

There is no clearly marked boundary.

Matter organises.
Complexity increases.
Information integrates.

And somewhere within this dynamic structure, experience appears.

Some scientists argue that consciousness is an emergent property – a result of sufficient complexity. Others propose that it arises from integrated information, as suggested by Giulio Tononi. Some, like neuroscientist Anil Seth, describe it as a controlled hallucination – the brain's best predictive model of sensory input.

These models attempt explanation.

But explanation is not yet equivalent.

To describe neural activity is not the same as describing what it feels like to see red or to hear music.

There remains a gap between mechanism and experience.

If the underlying structure of reality is probabilistic, relational, and mostly empty, how does it appear to us as stable, coloured, solid, and continuous? Where does definiteness arise? And more importantly – where do "you" arise within it?

Before we attempt to answer that, we must look more closely at the process through which reality becomes an experience.

If matter at its most fundamental level is described in terms of interaction and probability, and if the solidity of the world arises from structured forces rather than solid substance, then the next question becomes unavoidable: how does this structured interaction become an experience?

It is tempting to imagine that somewhere inside the body there is a silent observer – a small presence looking outward through the eyes, hearing through the ears, feeling through the skin. But biology offers no evidence for such a witness seated behind the senses.

There is no one inside the head peering out.

What exists instead is a nervous system – an extraordinarily complex network of approximately eighty–six billion neurons, each communicating through electrochemical signals. The eyes do not see in the way we casually describe. They detect photons. Photoreceptor cells in the retina respond to specific wavelengths of light. These responses are converted into electrical signals. Those signals travel along the optic nerve, are processed through multiple layers of neural circuitry, and are eventually integrated within the visual cortex.

At no point in this process does an image "enter" the brain as a miniature picture.

The brain does not receive a finished world.
It constructs one.

Neural systems detect differences – contrast, edges, motion, frequency, intensity. Separate regions process colour, shape, depth, and movement. These distributed signals are synchronised and integrated into a coherent scene. The world that appears stable and unified is the result of dynamic neural coordination.

The same is true for sound. Air vibrations reach the ear, causing the eardrum to move. These mechanical oscillations are converted into neural impulses. The brain interprets frequency and amplitude as pitch and volume. There is no inherent "music" in the air. There are pressure waves interpreted by neural systems.

Touch is not solidity itself. It is the detection of electromagnetic resistance, translated by sensory receptors in the skin into signals that the brain interprets as pressure, texture, or temperature.

Smell and taste are molecular interactions with receptor proteins, again converted into neural patterns.

In each case, external physical interaction becomes internal electrical activity.

And from that activity, a world appears.

The earlier questions now return.

As we have seen, if matter is structured interaction and perception is constructed from neural processing, then the reflection we see in the mirror is not a direct encounter with reality. It is the brain's best predictive model of light patterns correlated with a body.

The face in the mirror feels immediate and personal.

But what is actually present is a continuous loop of photons, neural activity, and interpretation.

The world appears.
The self appears – a perception of it that make us feel "me", or "I".
Both arise within process.

The constructed nature of perception becomes even clearer when we look at how vision develops.

This does not mean the world does not exist. It means that what is experienced as the world is a constructed model – a continuously updated representation built from sensory input and prior neural expectations.

The search continues only so long as there appears to be a seeker - a separate "someone" inside the head who lacks something and must go in search of it. Yet when we look carefully, this seeker becomes difficult to find. There are thoughts, sensations, memories, desires, fears. There is the feeling of being "me." But is there an actual entity behind them, apart from the thoughts that describe it? Or is the seeker itself another appearance within awareness - another object arising in consciousness?

If there is no separate seeker, then seeking changes its meaning. It is no longer one thing trying to reach another. The division between subject and object begins to soften. The world we experience is inseparable from the consciousness through which it appears. Objects are "there" only because there is a subject to know them; yet the subject itself, when examined, is found to be made only of passing experiences. This is close to what Gautama Buddha pointed toward in his teaching of Śūnyatā, or emptiness. Emptiness does not mean that nothing exists. It means that nothing exists independently, permanently, or by itself. The self is empty of a fixed essence. The world is empty of separate things. Everything arises together, dependent on everything else, like reflections in a mirror or waves upon the same sea.

Modern neuroscience increasingly supports this view. The brain does not passively receive reality; it actively predicts and updates. It generates internal models of the environment and refines them based on incoming data. Perception is less like a camera recording the world and more like a simulation being constantly corrected by sensory error signals.

The solidity of the chair, the colour of the sky, the continuity of time – all are features of this constructed model.

The earlier questions now return with new force.

If the physical world at its deepest level is structured interaction rather than solid substance, and if perception is the brain's constructed model of that interaction, then the sense of reality we inhabit is already one step removed from raw physical process. What appears as a stable external world is a neural interpretation of dynamic exchange.

There is no separate viewer located behind the eyes.

There is only process.

And yet, experience feels immediate. It feels cantered. It feels as though there is someone to whom it is happening.

That sense of centre will require careful examination.

But first, it is enough to recognise this: what is called reality is not accessed directly. It is mediated, processed, interpreted, and assembled.

The world as experienced is not raw existence. It is a constructed appearance arising from interaction.

David Chalmers famously called this the "hard problem" of consciousness.

Matter interacts.
Fields fluctuate.
Neurons fire.

And yet – experience.

We do not resolve this here.
We only recognise that the investigation has moved inward.

The world is not solid.
Matter is interaction.
The body is molecular structure.
And within this structure, experience is present.

The question now shifts. Not what the world is made of, but how is this experience constructed?

This insight has been emphasised by philosophers such as Daniel Dennett, who rejected the idea of a "Cartesian theatre" – a central location where a homunculus watches incoming data. Neuroscience finds no such observer.

Instead, distributed neural networks process patterns.

The brain constructs a model.

Modern cognitive science increasingly frames perception as predictive rather than reactive. According to the predictive processing framework – advanced by researchers such as Karl Friston and Anil Seth – the brain continuously generates hypotheses about the world. Sensory input is compared against predictions. Only prediction errors – deviations from expectation – are propagated upward.

In this view, perception is controlled hallucination.

Anil Seth writes that what we experience is the brain's best guess about the causes of sensory input. The world we perceive is not raw data, but a model stabilised by continuous error correction.

The brain does not access the world directly.
It receives delayed electromagnetic signals.
It integrates them across time windows.
It stabilises them into continuity.
It predicts.

What is striking is that long before neuroscience mapped distributed processing, contemplative traditions had already begun to question the apparent solidity of experience. The Buddha repeatedly pointed attention not to the objects of experience alone, but to the processes by which experience is assembled - contact, sensation, perception, mental formations, consciousness. What we take to be a stable world, and a stable one who knows it, is in Buddhist analysis a dependently arisen construction. The world of experience is not denied, but neither is it granted independent, self-existing certainty.

Advaita Vedanta moved in a different language but toward a similar destabilisation. Shankara described ordinary perception as conditioned by avidya - ignorance or misapprehension - in which the mind superimposes name, form, and separation upon the undivided real. What is ordinarily seen is not pure reality, but reality filtered through conceptual overlay. We do not merely see - we interpret, project, divide, and then take those divisions to be truth.

In Zen, this insight became even more immediate. Huang Po warned against trusting the discriminating mind, because the moment thought divides experience into subject and object, the original simplicity is lost. Sengcan, in the Hsin Hsin Ming, wrote that *the Great Way is not difficult for those who have no preferences/choice.* The problem is not the world itself, but the ceaseless mental movement that fragments what is whole into preferences, identities, and separate things. What is constructed then appears to us as given.

Kashmir Shaivism and the Vigyan Bhairav Tantra also suggest that ordinary perception is shaped by limitation. Consciousness, contracting into mind, experiences itself through fragmentation, sequence, and distinction. The practices do not ask us to acquire some new reality, but to see through the structuring activity that narrows the field of awareness into a world of separate objects and a separate experiencer.

Even modern spiritual teachers echoed this in simpler language. Krishnamurti insisted that the observer is the observed - that the one who claims to stand apart from experience is itself part of the movement being experienced. Nisargadatta Maharaj pointed again and again to the fact that the world one knows appears only with consciousness, and that the separate person taking ownership of experience is itself only another appearance within it. The error is not that experience occurs, but that thought inserts a centre and calls it "me".

Across these traditions, the suggestion is not identical in doctrine, but similar in direction: what appears immediate is already mediated; what appears solid is already interpreted; what appears to be reality itself is, at least in part, shaped by the structures through which it is known.

What you call reality is a controlled model.

Consider again the mirror.

When you look into a mirror, you say: "That is me."
But what actually occurs?

Photons reflect off your face. They strike the mirror. They reflect again into your eyes. Your retina converts light into electrical signals. Your visual cortex reconstructs spatial depth. Memory associates the pattern with prior self–images. Language assigns identity.

At no point does the brain encounter "you."
It encounters data.

It constructs recognition.

Recognition then becomes ownership.
Ownership becomes identity.

The image in the mirror feels immediate and self-evident. But it is the result of interpretation layered upon interpretation.

As philosopher Maurice Merleau–Ponty argued, perception is embodied. It is not a detached camera observing the world. It is an organism situated within an environment, interpreting through sensorimotor engagement.

You do not see the world as it is.

You see it as it is useful to your survival and action.

Newborn infants do not experience the world as adults do. Their visual acuity is limited. Colour discrimination develops over months as neural pathways mature. Depth perception emerges gradually. The brain learns to stabilise the world.

Developmental psychology shows that object permanence – the understanding that objects continue to exist when unseen – is not innate but acquired.

The stable world is learned.
Perception is trained.

The apparent solidity of experience emerges through repeated neural calibration.

Just as solidity emerges from quantum interaction, perceptual stability emerges from neural organisation.

Nothing appears fully formed.

Structure arises gradually.

Western philosophy wrestled with this for centuries.

John Locke distinguished between primary qualities (shape, motion) and secondary qualities (colour, taste), arguing that colour exists in the perceiver rather than the object.

Immanuel Kant went further. He proposed that space and time are not properties of things–in–themselves but forms of human intuition – structures imposed by the mind.

We do not perceive reality as it is.

We perceive phenomena shaped by cognitive categories.

Modern neuroscience gives empirical grounding to this philosophical insight.

The brain is not revealing reality.

It is modelling it.

Long before neuroscience, contemplative traditions articulated similar insights.

In early Buddhist analysis, experience is described not as contact with solid entities but as the arising of sensory events conditioned by contact between sense organs and their objects. The Buddha's framework of dependent origination suggests that perception arises dependent on conditions – not from a central perceiver.

Later Buddhist schools, such as Yogācāra, explicitly described experience as mind–constructed appearance.

Similarly, Advaita Vedanta questioned the independent reality of perceived phenomena, pointing to the role of cognition in shaping appearance.

These traditions did not have access to neural imaging or quantum theory.

Yet through introspective investigation, they reached structurally similar conclusions:

Experience is conditioned.
Perception is constructed.

There is no independent observer separate from experience.

We will explore these traditions more deeply later. For now, note the convergence.

Neuroscience finds no central locus of experience.

There is no identifiable "Self" centre in the brain where all information converges for a miniature observer to inspect.

Instead, experience arises from distributed processes.

Antonio Damasio distinguishes between the proto self (basic bodily mapping), the core self (momentary subjectivity), and the autobiographical self (narrative continuity). These are processes – not entities.

Thomas Metzinger argues that the self is a model generated by the brain – a transparent self–model that we mistake for a substance.

The feeling of being someone is a representational construct.

This does not mean it is false.
It means it is generated.

Why does perception feel stable?
Because the brain compresses complexity.

As we saw earlier, the physical world is dynamic – electrons fluctuating, atoms vibrating, galaxies rotating. But perception does not track quantum flux. It abstracts.

It reduces.
It simplifies.
It presents a manageable interface. If the self is a model – and the model is transparent – then who exactly has been living this life?

Donald Hoffman has argued that perception functions more like a user interface than a veridical representation. Just as desktop icons do not resemble the electrical circuitry of a computer, perceptual objects do not resemble the underlying physical reality.

The brain prioritises survival–relevant features.

The result is coherence – not completeness.

The present is not a universal slice of time. It is a constructed duration. Perception, similarly, is not a passive window. It is an active modelling process occurring within that duration. The world you experience now is:

- Delayed
- Interpreted
- Stabilised
- Predicted

This does not invalidate it. It contextualises it.

The Deeper Question Emerges

If perception is constructed…
If solidity is emergent…
If colour is neural interpretation…
If there is no central observer…

Then what is this persistent sense of "I" that claims ownership of experience?

Before we answer that, we must examine how identity is built from memory and narrative. Because just as perception is assembled from signals, the self may be assembled from experiences. And what feels most intimate – the sense of being someone – may be the most sophisticated construction of all.

WHAT REMAINS WHEN YOU ARE NOT

The question of the self or "me"/" I", has occupied both Eastern and Western thoughts for centuries, yet no stable agreement has ever been reached about what the "I" actually is.

When René Descartes declared, "*I think, therefore I am*" (cogito, ergo sum), he was attempting to locate certainty in an uncertain world. Everything could be doubted – the senses, the body, even the external world – but the act of doubting itself could not be denied. Thinking, he concluded, guaranteed the existence of a thinker. The "I" was anchored in the very activity of thought. Yet one might ask: was Descartes identifying a stable thinker behind thought, or merely recognising that thinking occurs? The distinction becomes crucial. One interpretation assumes a thinker behind thought – a stable subject that thinks and therefore *is*. Another interpretation, more radical, notices only that thinking is present and if there are not thoughts, there is no "*I*". The first reading strengthens identity. The second begins to question it.

In everyday language, the term appears simple. "I" refers to the person speaking. It signals identity, agency, continuity. It is the grammatical anchor of experience. Yet the apparent simplicity conceals a conceptual puzzle that has resisted resolution across philosophy, psychology, and neuroscience.

Is the self a substance?
A process?
A function?
A narrative?
A biological phenomenon?
Or something else entirely?

To understand the instability of the concept, it is useful to trace how Western thought has attempted to define it.

René Descartes sought certainty in an age of scepticism. Doubt everything, he argued – the senses, the world, even the body. But one thing cannot be doubted: the fact that doubt itself is occurring. The cogito appears to secure the self as indubitable. If thinking is present, then the thinker must exist. From this, Descartes inferred a thinking substance – res cogitans – distinct from extended physical matter.

The self, in this view, is a non–material entity whose essential attribute is thought.

This formulation profoundly shaped Western consciousness. It located identity in interiority. The Self became something private, internal, separate from the external world.

But Descartes' solution introduced a new problem: interaction. If mind and body are separate substances, how do they influence each other? How does an immaterial Self cause physical movement? This "mind–body problem" remains unresolved to this day.

More importantly for our enquiry, Descartes assumed that the existence of thinking implies the existence of a thinker as substance. The cogito secures thinking – but does it truly secure a substantial self beyond the activity itself?

That question would destabilise the entire framework.

David Hume approached the self differently. Rather than beginning with certainty, he began with observation. When he examined his own experience, he reported that he could never catch himself without a perception. He found sensations, impressions, thoughts – but never a Self– separate from them.

"I never can catch myself at any time without a perception and never can observe anything but the perception."

From this, Hume proposed what is now called the bundle theory of the self: the self is not a substance but a collection of perceptions in flux.

This was a radical destabilisation.

If the self is merely a bundle of experiences, then there is no fixed identity beneath them. Continuity becomes a function of memory and association.

Hume's view aligns strikingly with what modern cognitive science suggests: that the self may be an emergent pattern rather than an enduring entity.

Yet Hume's position felt psychologically unsettling. Without a stable self, what grounds moral responsibility? What grounds the identity across time?

Western philosophy oscillated again.

Immanuel Kant attempted to rescue coherence without reverting to substance dualism. He agreed with Hume that we do not encounter a self as object of perception. However, Kant argued that experience itself requires a unifying structure.

For perceptions to be organised into a coherent experience, there must be what he called the "*transcendental unity of apperception*" – a formal condition that allows experiences to be recognised as belonging together.

In simpler terms, Kant proposed that the self is not an object in experience but a necessary structural function that makes experience possible.

This move is subtle.
The self is not a thing.
But neither is it dispensable.
It becomes a condition of experience rather than a substance within it.

Yet Kant's self remains abstract. It cannot be observed directly. It cannot be described empirically. It is inferred as a logical requirement.

We are moving further away from the intuitive image of a solid inner person.

In psychology, William James introduced a crucial distinction between the "Me" and the "I."

The "Me" refers to the empirical self – body, possessions, social identity, psychological traits. It is the self that can be described.

The "I," by contrast, is the knower – the subject of experience.

James recognised that the "Me" changes continuously. What remains puzzling is the "I" that seems to observe those changes.

But even James hesitated to describe the "I" as a substance. He leaned toward viewing consciousness as a stream – a flowing process rather than a fixed entity.

Already, the solidity of the self was dissolving.

Sigmund Freud reframed the self again. For Freud, the ego was not a metaphysical centre but a mediator – balancing instinctual drives (id), moral constraints (superego), and external reality.

The ego became functional.

It was a regulatory system, not an immortal essence.

Carl Jung expanded this into layers – persona, shadow, collective unconscious – further fragmenting the idea of a single unified self.

Identity became psychological architecture.

Not metaphysical substance.

Jean–Paul Sartre pushed destabilisation further.

For Sartre, consciousness is not a thing. It is a nothingness – an openness in which phenomena appear. The ego, he argued, *does not reside inside consciousness. It exists in the world as an object among objects* – something we reflect upon.

The self, in this view, is constructed through projects, commitments, choices. There is no pre–given essence. Existence precedes essence.

The self becomes something continuously authored rather than inherently possessed.

Again, solidity dissolves.

Modern psychology and neuroscience often describe the self as a narrative construction.

Dan McAdams speaks of identity as an internalised life story. The brain integrates memories into coherent narratives that stabilise continuity.

Neuroimaging research identifies the Default Mode Network as heavily involved in self–referential thinking. When this network is active, individuals engage in autobiographical reflection, future simulation, and internal narration.

The self, in this framework, is a model the brain generates to organise behaviour and predict outcomes.

It is functional.
Adaptive.

But not independently existing.

Philosopher Daniel Dennett describes it as a "centre of narrative gravity" – similar to the centre of mass in physics. It is useful for explanation, but not a tangible object.

The metaphor is telling.

A centre of gravity is not a physical thing you can pick up. It is a calculated abstraction that describes how forces balance.

Is the Self similar?

Across Western thought, a pattern emerges.

The self is:

Not consistently described as substance.
Increasingly described as process or function.
Often treated as necessary for coherence.
Rarely located as a stable entity.

From Descartes' thinking substance to Hume's bundle, from Kant's transcendental unity to James' stream, from Freud's ego to Sartre's project, from narrative identity to neural models – the solidity of the "I" progressively thins.

What remains is a structural necessity or functional abstraction.

The intuitive inner person – the one sitting behind the eyes – finds less and less support.

Yet the feeling persists.

And this persistence is precisely what requires deeper examination.

If Western thought struggled to define the self philosophically, Eastern traditions approached the question through direct introspection and contemplative analysis.

Rather than asking, "What is the self?" they often asked, "Where is it? Can it be found?"

The difference in orientation is subtle but significant.

Western philosophy frequently attempted to stabilise the self conceptually. Eastern enquiry frequently attempted to dissolve it experientially.

Yet the results are not as simple as slogans suggest.

There was a time before language.

Before narrative.
Before identity.
Before the word "me."

An infant does not arrive in the world with a developed autobiography. There is sensation – warmth, hunger, sound, light – but there is no articulated owner of these experiences. There is no conceptual boundary separating "self" from "world." There is contact, but not yet identity.

Developmental psychology supports this. In the earliest months of life, sensory experience is primary. Vision is blurry. Motor coordination is incomplete. The nervous system is still calibrating itself to patterns of stimulation. Neural pathways are forming rapidly; synaptic density peaks in early childhood.

The infant feels.

But does not yet narrate.

Soon, a sound is repeated.

A name.

At first, it is just another auditory pattern. But gradually, through repetition, the sound becomes associated with bodily sensation. When the sound is spoken, attention shifts. Caregivers respond. The child is fed, lifted, comforted.

The name begins to anchor experience.

Language accelerates this process. Words are not merely labels; they are tools of categorisation. Through imitation and reinforcement, the child learns to associate pronouns: "mine," "yours," "me," "you."

Ownership emerges linguistically before it becomes conceptually firm.
"This is your toy."
"This is your mother."
"That is your bed."

Through repetition, relational boundaries solidify. The child learns to group sensations under a unifying reference point.

Identity begins as a grammatical necessity. But identity is not sustained by naming alone. It requires memory.

The hippocampus – a structure in the medial temporal lobe – plays a central role in forming episodic memories. These memories allow the organism to link past experiences into a coherent timeline.

Without memory, continuity dissolves.

Patients with severe amnesia, such as the well–documented case of Henry Molaison (known in neuroscience as H.M.), retained intelligence and personality traits but were unable to form new episodic memories. Their sense of self became fragmented across time.

Memory stitches moments together.

The "I" is the thread. Or appears to be.

Philosopher John Locke proposed that personal identity is grounded not in substance but in continuity of consciousness – especially memory. What makes you the same person today as yesterday is your capacity to remember being that person.

But memory itself is reconstructive.

Neuroscience shows that each act of remembering alters the memory slightly. The past is not replayed; it is reassembled.

Thus, the autobiographical self is dynamic.

It feels stable because reconstruction is seamless.

Over time, experiences accumulate.

School achievements.
Friendships.
Failures.
Successes.
Cultural values.
Social roles.

From this accumulation emerges a story.

"I am this kind of person."
"I come from here."
"I believe these things."

Over time this narrative thickens.

The child becomes a student, a friend, a son or daughter. Later perhaps a professional, a parent, a citizen of a country. Roles multiply, memories accumulate, and preferences take root.

A person appears to take shape.

This person seems to think, decide, judge, and choose. It develops ambitions and fears. It forms attachments and aversions. It remembers past experiences and projects itself into imagined futures.

It feels pride when praised and shame when criticised. It may develop loyalties to a nation, devotion to a religion, or commitment to a cause. It falls in love, builds families, pursues careers, dreams of success, fears failure.

The person becomes so vividly real that it appears to be the unquestioned centre of life.

Everything seems to revolve around it.

"My plans."
"My achievements."
"My suffering."
"My identity."

And because this person appears to be the one making decisions and experiencing the world, it is assumed to be the true owner of life.

Yet something remarkable happens when we pause and examine this "person" carefully.

Where exactly is it?

If we look into the body, we find organs, tissues, and cells.

If we examine the brain, we find networks of neurons exchanging electrical signals.

If we look into the mind, we encounter thoughts appearing and disappearing, memories surfacing and fading, emotions rising and dissolving.

But nowhere in this flowing activity do we find a stable entity that corresponds to the "person" we believe ourselves to be.

The identity that seems so solid in daily life turns out to be composed of fragments: memories, habits, learned responses, emotional patterns, cultural influences, and ongoing streams of thought.

What we call the "self" is not a fixed object hidden somewhere inside the mind. It is a dynamic pattern continuously reconstructed by the brain based on the data stored in the brain cells.

Each moment new thoughts arise, new perceptions appear, new

interpretations are formed. From this ongoing activity the mind generates the sense of a persistent centre – an "I" who seems to own the experiences.

Yet when we look directly for this centre, it cannot be found.

There are thoughts.
There are sensations.
There are emotions.
There are perceptions.

But the thinker of the thoughts, the owner of the sensations, the controller behind the experiences remains strangely absent.

The person who appears to be directing life may therefore be less like an independent entity and more like a narrative the mind continuously tells itself.

A useful story perhaps – one that helps organise memory, guide behaviour, and maintain social identity.

But a story, nonetheless.

And like all stories, it exists only as long as the telling continues.

Psychologist Dan McAdams describes identity as a life story – a narrative framework that integrates past, present, and anticipated future into coherence.

This narrative self is powerful. It guides decisions. It shapes expectations. It filters perception.

But it is constructed.

There is no physical structure in the brain labelled "self." There is activity – distributed networks coordinating memory, emotion, and future simulation.

"If the self is not real, then nothing matters."

But that is not what non–self means, and clarifying this actually strengthens the philosophical depth of your book.

Below is a section you can insert after the passage on the constructed identity, before transitioning toward consciousness.

Is the Self an Illusion?

At this point a natural objection may arise.

If the self we believe ourselves to be, cannot be found as a stable entity, does that mean the self is simply an illusion?

And if it is an illusion, does that imply that life itself is somehow meaningless or unreal?

Not quite.

The word illusion can be misleading. It often suggests something that does not exist at all, like a hallucination or a trick of the senses.

But the human self is not unreal in that sense.

The experiences that make up our lives are undeniably real. Thoughts occur. Emotions arise. Decisions are made. Relationships are formed. Joy and suffering are deeply felt.

What may be illusory is not the experiences themselves, but the assumption that there is a fixed and independent entity behind them.

To understand this distinction, it may help to consider a familiar example.

A whirlpool in a river appears to be a distinct object. It has a visible shape and a recognisable location. We can point to it and say, "There is a whirlpool."

Yet the whirlpool is not a separate thing existing apart from the river. It is simply a pattern formed by the movement of flowing water.

Remove the movement and the whirlpool disappears.

In much the same way, the self may be understood as a pattern emerging from the ongoing processes of brain, body, and environment.

Memories, sensations, emotions, and thoughts interact continuously. From this interaction arises a coherent narrative that gives the impression of a stable individual.

The self therefore functions as a useful organising centre within experience.

It allows the brain to maintain continuity across time, to plan for the future, to navigate social relationships, and to coordinate complex behaviour.

In this practical sense, the self is extremely real.

But when we search for the self as a distinct entity – something separate from the processes that produce it – we find nothing solid to grasp.

Like the whirlpool in the river, the self is not a thing.

It is a process.

Recognising this does not diminish the significance of life. On the contrary, it reveals something far more subtle and extraordinary.

Life is not being lived by a fixed entity controlling events from behind the scenes.

Instead, life unfolds as an intricate flow of experiences, actions, and relationships arising within a dynamic network of biological, psychological, and environmental processes.

The person we believe ourselves to be is part of that unfolding – not its owner.

This insight, far from being nihilistic, opens the door to a deeper understanding of human existence.

If the self is not a rigid and permanent entity, then many of the burdens we carry – the constant defence of identity, the fear of its loss, the endless comparison with others – begin to loosen their grip.

What remains is the simple fact of experience itself.

And this leads us to the next and perhaps most profound question of all.

If the self is a constructed narrative, and the body is a biological process, then what is the nature of the awareness in which all of this appears?

For most of human history, people have assumed that somewhere within the body there must exist a central observer – a thinker behind thoughts, a feeler behind feelings, a witness behind perception.

But as our investigation has unfolded, that centre has become increasingly difficult to locate.

Functional neuroimaging research identifies a set of regions often referred to as the Default Mode Network (DMN) – including the medial prefrontal cortex, posterior cingulate cortex, and angular gyrus. These regions are particularly active during self–referential thinking: recalling the past, imagining the future, reflecting on one's traits.

The brain, at rest, returns to story.

The narrative self is a pattern of neural activation.

Not an entity.

Philosophers such as Shaun Gallagher distinguish between the "minimal self" – the immediate sense of embodied presence – and the "narrative self" – the extended autobiographical identity.

The minimal self is pre–reflective. It is the felt sense of being here, now. It does not require language.

The narrative self is constructed across time.

When you say, "I am a teacher," "I am a parent," "I am successful," you are invoking narrative layers.

Both feel personal.
Both feel immediate.
Yet neither is fixed.

The minimal self depends on continuous sensory integration. Disrupt that integration – through neurological injury or certain psychiatric conditions – and the sense of embodied ownership can fragment.

The narrative self depends on memory and social reinforcement. Change environment, culture, or belief system, and identity reshapes.

Stability emerges from reinforcement.
Not from substance.
Identity does not develop in isolation.

Family, education, religion, nationality – all contribute.

"You are Australian."
"You are American."
"You are Christian."
"You are a scholar."
"You are successful."
"You are not enough."

These statements, repeated across years, embed into the narrative framework. They become filters through which experience is interpreted.
The self–model becomes socially co–authored.

This is why identity feels unquestionable. It has been rehearsed thousands of times. Identity is not purely cognitive. It is affective.

Pride. Shame. Desire. Fear.

These emotions reinforce the self–model. The amygdala and limbic system contribute to the tagging of experiences as significant. Events that threaten identity trigger physiological arousal.

Criticism feels personal.
Loss feels existential.
Achievement feels expansive.

The self is emotionally defended because it is neurologically reinforced.

Yet this defence does not prove its solidity.

It proves its importance to survival and social cohesion.

Early Buddhist thought articulated a framework known as the Five

Aggregates (skandhas):

Form (physical body)
Sensation (feeling tone)
Perception (recognition)
Mental formations (thought, intention)
Consciousness (awareness of object)

According to this analysis, what we call a "person" is a dynamic aggregation of these processes. There is no permanent, independent self– underlying them.

This is not a denial of experience.

It is a denial of fixed essence.

The Buddha did not deny the self as a rhetorical gesture. He analysed experience.

Form.
Feeling.
Perception.
Mental formations.
Consciousness.

These five aggregates arise dependently. None remains fixed. None qualifies as permanent. None can be grasped as "This is me."

The self, then, is not destroyed – it is seen through.
To illustrate this, the Buddha offered a simple image.

A lute produces sound when strings are tuned, wood intact, fingers moving, and musician present. Remove one condition, and the sound ceases.

Where is the sound located?

Not in the wood.
Not in the strings.
Not in the musician.

It arises when conditions meet.

Likewise, what we call "self" arises when body, sensation, perception, and consciousness operate together. It functions. It appears. But it has no independent core.

The sound is real while playing – but it has no substance.

Nāgārjuna extended this analysis through the doctrine of śūnyatā – emptiness.

Emptiness does not mean nothingness. It means lack of independent existence. Yet, emptiness does not mean nothingness. It means that nothing possesses independent, permanent existence in itself. Science, strangely enough, gestures in a similar direction. Atoms join to form molecules; molecular bonds give rise to solids, liquids, gases, and all the visible structures of the world. Nothing stands entirely alone. Everything exists through conditions, relations, and mutual dependence - including what we call a person. Yet this is not quite what the Buddha meant by emptiness. He was not speaking of empty space within atoms, nor suggesting that life is meaningless, valueless, or void in a nihilistic sense. Emptiness does not mean that things do not exist. It means they do not exist in the fixed, separate, and enduring way the mind assumes. Hence Avalokiteśvara's uncompromising insight in the Heart Sutra: "Form is emptiness; emptiness is form." The world is not denied. It is released from the false solidity we project upon it.

Everything exists dependently.

If the Self existed inherently, it would not change. It would not age. It would not fluctuate. Yet what we call "I" shifts continuously.

Thus, the self is designation – useful, but empty of intrinsic being.

The ego appears solid only because its dependent nature is not examined.

In the Bhagavad Gita, Krishna speaks of the ātman as unborn and undying – untouched by weapons, fire, or decay. But this teaching is often misunderstood.

Krishna simultaneously says that actions are performed by the gunas of nature, while the deluded self believes, "I am the doer."

The emphasis is not on strengthening personal identity, but on dissolving identification with action.

Over time, devotional interpretation personalised the teaching into "my soul."

But the original structural insight destabilises egoic agency. It separates the witnessing principle from psychological ownership.

The one who says, "I act," is already mistaken.

Advaita Vedanta proceeds by negation.

Not this body.
Not these thoughts.
Not these emotions.

Each identification is examined and set aside.

Ramana Maharshi condensed the method into a single enquiry: "Who am I?"

When the "I" is searched for directly, what is found?

A thought.
An arising sense.
A movement.

And like all movements, it subsides.

The "I–thought" itself is transient.

What remains cannot be objectified.

Zen is less analytical and more surgical.

Hui–Neng declared that originally there is not a single thing. If nothing has inherent existence, what exactly is there to polish?

The famous Sēngcàn and Huike encounter illustrates this directly.

"*Sēngcàn was in search for a master and found Huike. Feeling burdened by guilt and resulting illnesses, he asked the master to free him of his sins so that he could enter Zen.*

Huike replied, "Bring me your sin and I will absolve you."

Sēngcàn searched. For days. He could not find them. Then one day, suddenly, it dawned on him. He hurried back to the master. He said, "When I look for it, I cannot find it.". What he called "sin" existed only as thoughts in his mind. The master replied: "There. I have freed you."

Zen does not philosophise about the self. It reveals its absence through direct confrontation and self-realisation.

Sufi mysticism speaks in warmer tones, but its implication is equally radical. The ego is described as a veil – not substance, but obscuration.

As long as even a subtle strand of "I am this" persists, separation persists.
Rumi suggested that vanity and self–praise survive as long as a fragment of personal being remains.

Ibn Arabi went further. The individual "I" has no independent existence; it is a locus of manifestation within Unity. The mistake lies not in appearance, but in mistaking reflection for source.

Bayazid al–Bistami once asked a child carrying a candle, "Where did the light come from?"

The child blew it out and asked, "Where has it gone?"

The saint fell silent.

The mind seeks origin and destination. The ego claims to know. But the very structure of knower collapses under examination.

Taoist imagery avoids metaphysics altogether.

The ego is compared to a monkey swinging from branch to branch – from desire to desire, from thought to thought.

Peace is not achieved by controlling the monkey. It comes from ceasing to follow it. When attention rests in stillness, the movement continues – but the identification weakens.

Eventually, even the sense of being the watcher dissolves.
In the Vigyan Bhairav Tantra, Shiva does not describe ultimate reality.

He provides methods.

Observe the pause between inhalation and exhalation.
Notice the instant between two thoughts.
Rest in the gap before a desire forms.
In these intervals, no self is found.
There is awareness.

But no narrative centre claiming ownership.

The "I" appears intermittent – stitched together by continuous thought. Between thoughts, there is no thinker. The continuity we attribute to the self is an interpretive overlay.

Across traditions – Buddhist, Vedantic, Zen, Sufi, Taoist, Tantric – the pattern converges.

The ego cannot withstand sustained enquiry.
It is movement mistaken for entity.
Layer mistaken for kernel.
Veil mistaken for separation.
Reflection mistaken for source.

Yet even after this examination, the sense of self returns.

The enquiry, therefore, must deepen.

Across these traditions – Buddhist, Vedantic, Zen, Sufi – a pattern appears:

The psychological ego is not ultimate.
Identification with body and thought creates suffering.
Direct enquiry dissolves assumed identity.
What remains is not easily captured in conceptual language.

Yet there are differences.

Buddhism avoids positing an eternal Self.
Advaita affirms pure awareness as ultimate reality.
Zen avoids metaphysical framing.
Sufism speaks relationally of divine union.
The vocabulary shifts.

The direction converges.

It is important not to collapse distinctions.

Some traditions speak of soul.
Some deny soul.
Some affirm awareness.
Some emphasise emptiness.

But if we look beneath terminology, a structural move is consistent:

The self that claims ownership – the thinker, the doer, the controller – cannot withstand sustained enquiry.

The remaining question is subtle.

When the personal "I" loosens, does anything remain?

Is there awareness without owner?
Is there emptiness without nihilism?
Is there functioning without identity?

Before answering, we must proceed carefully.

We have surveyed philosophy and mysticism.

Now we must turn inward.
Not to adopt doctrine.
But to examine directly.

Having surveyed philosophy and contemplative traditions, a natural question arises:

If so many thinkers across cultures have struggled to locate a permanent self, why does the sense of "I" remain so convincing?

Why does it feel central, solid, unquestionable?
The answer lies not in metaphysics, but in mechanism.

The self persists because it is reinforced continuously – cognitively, emotionally, socially, and biologically.

The most powerful reinforcement mechanism is language.
Language requires subjects and objects.

"I see."
"I think."
"I feel."
"I did."

Every sentence subtly reaffirms a centre.

The grammar of most human languages encodes agency. Actions must be assigned to someone. Even impersonal events are often personified.

Through repetition from childhood, this grammatical structure becomes ontological assumption. Because we speak in first–person terms, we infer a first–person entity.

But grammar does not prove substance. It organises communication.
Over time, linguistic tagging creates continuity. The name given in childhood becomes attached to memories, achievements, failures. The word refers to a growing archive. The archive becomes identity.

The self becomes a narrative anchor.

Secondly, memory deepens the illusion of continuity.

Without memory, identity collapses. Severe amnesia demonstrates this clearly. When autobiographical memory is disrupted, the sense of being a continuous person fragments.

But memory is not playback. It is reconstruction.

Each act of remembering subtly alters the memory itself. Neuroscience shows that memories are re–encoded upon retrieval. The past is rebuilt, not replayed.

Yet because the reconstruction is seamless, it feels stable. The self becomes the thread connecting reconstructed episodes.

But the thread is conceptual. It exists in narrative cohesion. From the emotional reinforcement point of view, cognition alone does not sustain identity.

Emotion fuels it.
Pride reinforces success.
Shame reinforces failure.
Fear protects self–image.
Desire expands aspiration.

The amygdala tags experiences as significant. Emotion binds memory to identity. The stronger the emotional charge, the deeper the identification.

Criticism feels like an attack on being, not merely on opinion.
Praise feels like expansion of self.
The self–model becomes emotionally defended territory.
To question it triggers resistance.

Beneath cognitive and emotional reinforcement lies a deeper force: fear.

Fear of insignificance.
Fear of death.
Fear of non–existence.

The idea of a stable "I" provides psychological shelter.
If there is a centre, then life has owner.
If there is owner, then life has meaning.

The dissolution of self can feel like annihilation. Even conceptually entertaining non–self can evoke subtle panic.

This existential tension explains why doctrines of eternal soul persist. They stabilise anxiety.

The self is not merely an idea.
It is a psychological defence.

Then, from a neuroscientific perspective, the self–model enhances predictive efficiency.

The brain constantly predicts sensory input. Having a stable reference model of "this body in this environment" reduces computational load. The organism tracks itself as an entity moving through space.

This is adaptive.

Without self–modelling, coordination would degrade.

The problem arises not at the level of functional modelling, but at the level of metaphysical assumption.

A model is taken as entity.
Utility becomes ontology.
Identity is reinforced socially.

"You are responsible."
"You are successful."
"You disappointed me."
"You are talented."

From childhood onward, the self is mirrored by others. Social feedback shapes narrative identity. Over time, external reinforcement becomes internalised voice.

The internal narrator often echoes parental or cultural tone.

The self becomes co–authored.

And because society requires stable persons for moral and legal systems, identity is institutionally stabilised. Contracts, laws, reputations – all depend on persistent self–reference. The illusion becomes civilisational infrastructure.

Now observe the paradox.

The self is:

Linguistically reinforced
Memory-stitched
Emotionally defended
Fear-protected
Predictively useful
Socially co-authored

Every layer supports it.

Yet none of these layers establishes it as independent substance.
The Self functions. But function does not imply metaphysical solidity.

This is the critical distinction.

At this stage, the enquiry becomes delicate. Conceptually, one may understand that the "I" is constructed. One may agree intellectually that identity is narrative. One may accept that thoughts arise without central author. But intellectual agreement is not dissolution.

The mechanism continues. The identification persists. To move beyond theory, something subtler must occur:

The "I" must observe itself.
Not as idea.
As immediate experience.

How does the sense of "me" arise in this moment?

Where is it located?
What happens if it is not reinforced?

The next movement of this chapter approaches that threshold.

But before stepping into experiential territory, we must stabilise something crucial.

This enquiry is not nihilism. It is not self-negation. It is not psychological erasure. Function continues. Practical identity remains. What softens is ownership.

The shift is from:

"I am doing life."
to
"Life is happening."

This distinction is subtle.

It cannot be forced.
It must be seen.
At this stage of the enquiry, something subtle begins to shift.

We have examined the self philosophically.
We have analysed it psychologically.

We have traced its construction through language and memory.
We have seen how traditions across cultures destabilise its solidity.

Conceptually, the argument is strong. Yet something persists. The feeling of being someone remains. It remains not as theory, but as immediacy. There is still a sense that there is an "I" here – reading, evaluating, agreeing or disagreeing. This is where the enquiry must turn inward.

Not to adopt doctrine. But to observe directly.

J. Krishnamurti repeatedly articulated a sentence that, at first glance, seems paradoxical:

"The observer is the observed."
It is easy to treat this as mystical rhetoric. But examined carefully, it is structural.

Consider a simple example.

Anger arises.

Immediately, there appears to be two:

– The anger.
– The "I" who is angry.
The "I" claims ownership: I am angry.
But what is this "I" separate from anger?

If one looks closely in the moment of anger, what is found?
There is physiological arousal.
There are thoughts.
There is tension.
There is memory of grievance.

The "I" that claims to be angry is itself composed of those elements. It is not outside them. The observer of anger is not separate from anger. It is the continuation of anger in conceptual form. The division between observer and observed may itself be constructed.

Psychologically, division creates control. If anger is separate from "me," then "I" can suppress it, manage it, overcome it. But if the observer is structurally the same as the observed – if the "I" is itself a movement of thought – then division collapses.

This does not eliminate anger. It eliminates the illusion of a controller separate from it.

This insight is not mystical.

It is direct.

The thinker is thought.
The experiencer is experience in motion.
The doer is action interpreted narratively.

When examined in real time, the separation softens.
At first, this is understood intellectually.

One may recognise:
Thoughts arise without being summoned.
Emotions surge without deliberate creation.
Identity shifts depending on context.

The "I" appears as a summary label for complex processes.
This stage is important.

Conceptual clarity destabilises blind belief.

But conceptual clarity alone does not dissolve identification. The mechanism of "selfing" continues automatically. Something else must occur.

When attention turns inward without judgment – simply observing the sense of "me" – an interesting phenomenon occurs. The "I" cannot be located as object.

There are sensations in the body.
There are thoughts referring to self.
There may be a subtle contraction in the chest or head.

But the solid entity is not found. Instead, there is process. This is not a philosophical conclusion. It is experiential.

The self cannot be located because it is not a thing. It is an activity. An activity of identification.

When this is seen repeatedly – not believed but observed – identification begins to loosen.

Function continues.
Speech continues.
Work continues.
Relationships continue.
But the psychological contraction softens.

The sense of being the central author of life relaxes.

There is still practical identity – a name, a role, responsibilities. But the heavy ownership begins to dissolve.

Life continues.
The claim of possession weakens.
This is why earlier we clarified:

Here:
This is not nihilism.
This is not passivity.
This is not withdrawal from life.

A minimal functional identity remains – necessary for coordination.

But it no longer drives existence as a defended centre.

When identification loosens, something surprising may occur. Action becomes simpler. Without the constant narrative reinforcement of "me," responses arise more fluidly.

Zen refers to this as spontaneity.

Taoism describes it as wu–wei (*wuwei*)– effortless action – Tao abides in stillness, yet nothing is left undone.

Modern psychology calls similar states "flow."

In these states, activity happens without heavy self–reference. The organism functions efficiently. The doer is less prominent. The idea of being in control diminishes – yet responsiveness improves.

However, the paradox deepens:
When the ego relaxes, functioning does not collapse. It often becomes clearer.

What Remains?

Now we approach the delicate edge.

If the observer is the observed…
If the thinker is thought…
If the "I" is an activity rather than an entity…

What remains?

There is awareness.
But not as possession.
There is experiencing.
But not as owner.

This is where language begins to strain. Zen sometimes calls it "no-mind." Advaita calls it the Self – but not personal self. Buddhism refrains from naming it. Sufis speak of annihilation and union.

Each tradition gestures toward something beyond identity – yet none can define it without turning it into concept.

So, we pause here.
We do not assert.
We observe.
The enquiry has dismantled what the "I" is not.

The question that now emerges is not theoretical.

It is immediate:
If not this "I," then what?

At this point in the enquiry, the mind may still search for something solid.

If the self is not an entity, then what exactly are we? The Buddha once offered a simple analogy.

Imagine a lute.

When its strings are tuned, the wood intact, the player skilled, and the fingers in motion – sound arises.

Where does the sound exist?

Is it in the wood alone?
In the strings alone?
In the musician's fingers?

Remove any one of these conditions, and the sound ceases.

The sound does not reside independently in any component.

It arises when conditions meet.

In the same way, what we call "self" arises when body, sensation, perception, memory, and consciousness operate together. It is not found in the body alone. Not in feeling alone. Not in thought alone. Not in awareness alone.

It is a coordination.
A process.
A conditional emergence.

When conditions shift – in deep sleep, in unconsciousness, in neurological injury – the sense of self alters or disappears entirely. Nothing metaphysical leaves. Nothing eternal departs. The coordination changes.

The "I" is like the music.
Real while playing.
Absent when conditions cease.
Not located anywhere independently.

This analogy is neither nihilistic nor mystical.
It is descriptive.

The sound exists – but not as substance. The Self functions – but not as independent entity. When this is understood, something subtle occurs. The urgency to defend a centre diminishes.

Action continues – just as music continues while conditions support it.
Responsibility remains – because actions have consequences within the field of conditions.

Compassion deepens – because the boundaries between "self" and "other" soften.

What dissolves is not functioning.
What dissolves is psychological contraction. There is still perception. Still decision. Still movement. But without the heavy insistence: "This is me. This is mine. I am the doer."

Life continues. Ownership relaxes.

This is not passivity. The lute still plays. This is not withdrawal. Music continues. This is not self-negation. It is recognition of conditional emergence.

A small, practical identity remains for coordination – a name, a role, a signature. Society requires it. The body requires it.

But inwardly, the centre is lighter.

Less defended.
Less burdened.
And perhaps – quieter.

We have now seen:

The self cannot be located philosophically.
It dissolves under Buddhist analysis.
It is negated in Zen immediacy.
It is transcended in Advaita enquiry.
It collapses when observer and observed are examined.
It arises conditionally like sound from a lute.

If this is so –
Then what is awareness itself?
Is it also conditional?
Is it fundamental?

Is it relational?
Is it emergent?

We do not answer that here. The enquiry deepens in the next part.

Even after seeing that the Self arises conditionally – like sound from a lute – the mechanism does not immediately stop.

Thought continues to leap.
Desire shifts.
Memory reasserts.

Ancient Taoist texts describe the ego as restless movement – like a monkey swinging from branch to branch, grasping at sensations, identities, ambitions. One desire barely satisfied gives way to another. The senses fascinate. The mind chases. This restlessness creates the illusion of centre. Where there is continuous movement, the mind assumes there must be a mover. But if one remains still – attentive – the movement is seen without identifying with it.

Lao Tzu's gesture was simple: return to the centre. Not by suppressing movement, but by ceasing to follow it. Eventually, even the sense of being the watcher softens.

Not the monkey controlled.
Not the monkey killed.
Simply not grasped.
Other teachers have used different metaphors.

The ego is like an onion.

Layer upon layer:

Name.
Family role.
Profession.
Beliefs.
Memories.
Opinions.
Traumas.
Achievements.

Each layer feels substantial. Each one says, "This is me." But when examined and peeled away, no solid kernel is found at the centre. Sri Ramakrishna and many Buddhist teachers used this imagery to illustrate the absence of an independent core. What remains when the layers are removed is not a hidden entity – but openness.

The disappointment of not finding a kernel is precisely the point. The self was assumed. It was never located.

In Sufi teaching, the ego is described not as substance but as veil. It does not create separation by existing independently; it creates separation by obscuring. As long as even a thin strand of "I am this" persists, self–reference subtly continues. Vanity, comparison, self–concern survive in refined form.

Rumi wrote that so long as a fragment of "you" remains, the distance remains.

This is not annihilation in the dramatic sense.

It is transparency.
The veil becomes thinner.
Eventually, what was thought to be the centre is revealed as reflection.

Ibn Arabi described the human "I" as a locus of manifestation – not independent being, but a reflection within the Unity of Being. The ego appears solid only because it mistakes reflection for source.

The illusion is not that the world appears.
The illusion is that it appears to someone separate.

There is a story of Bayazid al–Bistami encountering a child carrying a lit candle at night.

Playfully, he asked, "Where did this light come from?"

The child extinguished the flame and replied, "Tell me where it has gone."

The saint was struck silent.

The mind seeks origin and destination.
But what we call beginning and ending may be conceptual overlays on

process.

The ego assumes knowing. The collapse comes not from acquiring knowledge – but from seeing the limits of the knower.

Across Taoist, Vedantic, Buddhist, and Sufi expressions, a pattern emerges. The ego is not attacked as enemy. It is seen as misidentification. It is movement mistaken for entity. It is layering mistaken for core. It is veil mistaken for distance. It is reflection mistaken for source.

When this is seen, gently and repeatedly, something relaxes.

Not violently.
Not dramatically

.

Simply the insistence that there must be a solid centre weakens.

Life continues.
The body breathes.
Thought arises.
Speech occurs.

But the psychological contraction – the need to defend, accumulate, assert – softens.

This is not self-erasure.
It is decentralisation.
The music still plays.

But no instrument claims authorship.

And yet, even now, the sense of "I" remains. It will rise again in the next thought. It will say, "I understand this." It will claim ownership of insight.

The enquiry is not finished.

And yet, even now, the sense of "I" persists. It will rise in the next thought and quietly say, "I understand this." It will claim ownership of insight, of clarity, of realisation. The very movement that has just been examined attempts to appropriate the examination itself. The self–model does not disappear because it has been analysed; it reconstitutes itself in subtler forms.

The enquiry, therefore, is not complete.

If the "I" can dissolve conceptually yet continue functionally…
If it can loosen without life collapsing…
If it can be seen through and yet still appear…
Then the question deepens.

What exactly is this "I" in lived experience?
How does it operate moment to moment?
And can it be observed directly – not as theory, but as immediate fact?

The next step is no longer philosophical.

It is experiential.

Up to this point, the instability has been external. Light does not behave as intuition suggests. Time is not universal. Matter dissolves into fields and probabilities.

But the world still appears solid.

The sun still rises. The body still moves. The present still feels immediate.

The destabilisation has occurred in theory. The experience remains unchanged.

So, the next question becomes unavoidable:

If reality is structurally unstable at the physical level, why does it appear so stable in experience?

This is where the enquiry turns inward.

There is no one sitting behind the eyes watching the world. There is no internal observer looking out from a control room inside the skull. What exists instead is a biological system continuously constructing a model of its surroundings.

Every sight, sound, taste, and sensation is an interpretation. The brain does not passively receive reality. It actively predicts it.

Modern neuroscience increasingly describes perception not as reception but as controlled hallucination. The brain generates a model of the world and constantly updates it based on incoming sensory signals. What we call "seeing" is the brain's best guess about what is out there.

And most of the time, that guess works.

But it is still a guess.

THE BODY–SOUL CONUNDRUM

For many, the prospect of an enduring essence surviving bodily dissolution is both a profound mystery and a source of deep psychological comfort. This duality fits seamlessly into theological frameworks of justice: heaven and hell, reward and retribution, while providing a metaphysical foundation for social orders built upon the binaries of good and evil.

While cultural vocabularies diverge, the underlying intuition remains strikingly consistent. Plato famously conceptualised the soul as a *pre–existing entity*, a charioteer temporarily tasked with tethering the unruly horses of physical desire. In the Christian tradition, the soul is a divinely created, morally accountable spark destined for an eternal fate of salvation or loss. Islamic thought further nuances this by distinguishing between Ruh–the pure, divine breath–and Nafs, the evolving self in need of purification. Meanwhile, the Upanishads point toward Atman: an eternal, unchanging witness that is ultimately indistinguishable from Brahman, the absolute ground of reality. Even in the broader Greek tradition, the Psyche served as the vital "animating principle," the invisible breath that transforms mere matter into a living person.

And yet, even within these traditions, the soul has never meant quite the same thing.

For Thomas Aquinas, the soul was the “form” of the body – not a ghost floating inside it, but the principle that makes a body alive rather than inert. For Descartes, the soul – or thinking substance – was entirely distinct from extended matter. For Immanuel Kant, the soul could not be known as an object of experience at all; it was a necessary postulate of reason, a condition for moral accountability. Alan Watts later reframed the entire issue, suggesting that what we call the "soul" may be less an individual possession and more an expression of the total universe appearing locally – like a wave on the ocean mistaking itself for something separate from water.

The difficulty begins when soul is interpreted primarily through the lens of personal identity. In many religious and philosophical traditions - especially those shaped by strong ideas of individual judgement, heaven, hell, and personal salvation - the soul is imagined as something like the permanent inner person, the one who remains the same and continues after death. From within that framework, teachings on no-self naturally appear contradictory, because they seem to threaten the continuity of the individual, or the individual identity. But perhaps this is precisely where confusion begins. The separate "I" - the one that says my life, my beliefs, my destiny, my soul - is itself a mental construction, woven from memory, emotion, and the continuing thought-based narrative. It does not even fully know what it is, yet it assumes it can possess something ultimate.

The contradiction is subtle but profound: the ego seeks salvation for itself, while the very truth being pointed to may require seeing through the ego altogether. If there is something real that survives, it would not need the story of a person in order to be what it is. The soul, in that deeper sense, cannot belong to the "I," because the "I" is precisely what does not endure. This is not easily understood in the context of everyday life; we plan, we act, we make decisions, we try to control the life around us – think we have a huge responsibility towards the family, the society, the nation, and people all around us. And then to think that the one doing all the actions and making decisions is not real? It is not easy. The mind tells you that it can solve problems by thinking and logic alone, that it can control life and find answers. It is a very powerful feeling, a powerful thought. Yet, when we look closely, the thinking mind does none of that. What it accumulates is word-based information. Thinking does not provide an experience. It may create an imagination but fails to live in a true experience. Even to truly fall in love, you have to let go of yourself. No thought exist. If a thought enters, love disappears. Then love is only a transaction, like everything else in life. There are often glimpses. There are moments when you are not thinking anything, not worried about anything, not planning anything, and not interpreting anything. You are suddenly filled with an unmistakable sense of serenity and calm. Those are rare moments. They do not last long. But they can. Chinese Zen calls it *Wu-Nian* (無念, wúniàn) – no mind, no thought. Just being.

Yet, the concept of soul does not go away. As Ramana Maharishi points out, it is not whether soul exists or not. The real question is "who" is the one that thinks that the soul exists? "Who" is asking the question? Who is this "I"?

The mystics spoke differently. Meister Eckhart declared that the deepest ground of the soul is identical with the ground of God – not something personal but something without image or form. St. Augustine wrestled inwardly and found not a separate entity but a depth of interiority – "*more inward to me than my inmost self.*" George Gurdjieff, on the other hand, suggested that the soul is not given automatically at birth; it must be consciously developed, crystallised through awareness and effort.

In Islamic philosophy, Ibn Sina – Avicenna – argued through reason that the soul must be independent of the body, offering his famous "floating man" thought experiment: imagine a man suspended in air, deprived of sensory input – he would still affirm his own existence. Yet Sufi masters like Ibn Arabi dissolved even this affirmation into a deeper unity – *Wahdat al-Wujud* – the Unity of Being, where the individual self is but a reflection of the One reality. Rumi warned that as long as a "strand of you" remains, the veil persists.

Guru Nanak sang of the soul as light merging back into Light. Ramana Maharshi turned the enquiry inward – asking relentlessly, "Who am I?" – until even the seeker dissolved. Adi Shankaracharya declared the Self unborn, untouched, identical with Brahman – but insisted it is not the ego, not the thinker, not the doer.

And so, the word "soul" stretches across metaphysics, devotion, philosophy, poetry, and psychology. Sometimes it means an immortal individual essence. Sometimes it means pure awareness. Sometimes it means divine spark. Sometimes it means pattern. Sometimes it means nothing separate at all.

The word remains. The meanings multiply.

Despite the diversity of symbols and metaphors, a common thread persists: the body is temporary; the soul is not. The body decays; the soul survives. The body belongs to earth; the soul belongs elsewhere. This idea – body–soul duality – is perhaps one of humanity's most enduring intuitions. The body is seen as a vehicle, the soul as the driver. The body as garment, the soul as wearer. The body as instrument, the soul as musician.

Scriptures declare the soul unborn, undying, eternal, unchanging.

Teachers repeat it.
Devotees recite it.
Movements are built around it.

And yet, in ordinary speech, the language shifts.

"My soul needs purification."
"My soul is evolving."
"My soul will progress."
"My soul will reunite with God."
"My soul will travel."

If the soul is eternal, unchanging, and pure, does it perform actions? If it does not act, then who accumulates? If it acts, how does it remain untouched? If it is omnipresent and beyond time, how does it travel to heaven, hell, or another birth? Movement implies location; location implies limitation.

And what exactly is evolving?

If the soul is eternal and unchanging, it cannot improve.
If it can improve, it was incomplete.
If it was incomplete, it was not absolute.
If it is absolute, it cannot move toward anything.

The contradiction is not subtle. It is visible – almost embarrassingly visible – yet it remains largely unquestioned.

And in Buddhism – most radically – there is no eternal soul at all. The Buddha compared the person to a chariot assembled from parts. Remove the wheels, the axle, the frame – where is the chariot? Likewise, remove form, sensation, perception, mental formations, consciousness – where is the self? Nagarjuna later pressed this further: nothing possesses inherent, independent existence; all arises dependently.

Yet even where soul is denied, continuity is not dismissed. There is process, causation, unfolding – but not a fixed entity.

In the Bhagavad Gita, on the battlefield of Kurukshetra, Arjuna stands paralysed by moral conflict. He sees teachers, cousins, and friends arrayed before him. To fight is to kill. To refuse is to betray duty. In that moment of hesitation, Krishna speaks not of strategy, but of life and death themselves. He says:

न जायते म्रियते वा कदाचिन्
नायं भूत्वा भविता वा न भूयः।
अजो नित्यः शाश्वतोऽयं पुराणो
न हन्यते हन्यमाने शरीरे॥

(Bhagavad Gita 2.20)

"*The Self is never born, nor does it die.*
Having once existed, it never ceases to be.
Unborn, eternal, everlasting, ancient –
It is not slain when the body is slain."

The declaration is absolute. The Self is unborn. It does not come into being. It does not pass away. Weapons cannot cut it. Fire cannot burn it. Water cannot wet it. Wind cannot dry it. Yet, it has been immensely misunderstood.

The moment the ego hears the word soul, it performs the same action it learned in childhood. Just as it once said my toy, my bed, my food, my parents, my life, it now says "my soul". The pattern is identical - thought hears a word, forms an association, and turns it into ownership. But if the so-called "I" cannot even clearly locate or define itself, on what basis can it claim ownership of something as subtle as soul? The "I" is itself only a construct - a continuity assembled from memory, sensation, emotional residues, and repeated thought patterns. It is not a stable knower, but an after-image created by the brain's ongoing organisation of experience. Thought can name, compare, remember, and claim, but thought does not itself experience. Experience happens, and thought arrives afterwards to say, "*This happened to me.*" In that sense, the ego does not discover the soul; it appropriates the idea of soul and folds it into the same old structure of possession and identity. This is one of the deepest forms of ignorance - the attempt of a mental construct to own what, in its truest sense, cannot belong to any construct at all.

If taken seriously, this Self is beyond time, beyond change, beyond decay.

And here, quietly, something important happens.

If the Self is unborn and undying, who stands on the battlefield?

If it cannot be slain, who fears death?
If it is eternal and untouched, who acts and who suffers?

When Krishna speaks to Arjuna about the ātman or self, the word is often translated into English as "soul." Over centuries this translation has shaped, rightly or wrongly, how many people understand the teaching.

The term soul, particularly in Western languages, usually suggests a personal entity – something that belongs to an individual, carries their identity, and continues to exist after death as the same person.

But this interpretation may miss a subtle and important distinction in the original philosophical context.

Krishna is not describing the continuation of the psychological personality that humans normally identify with – the collection of memories, habits, preferences, fears, ambitions, and roles that form what we ordinarily call a "person." That personality is precisely what our earlier enquiry has shown to be fluid and constructed.

The ātman referred to in the Bhagavad Gita appears to point to something more fundamental.

It refers to the underlying awareness within which the changing activities of mind and body arise.

Thoughts appear within it.
Sensations arise within it.
Memories and emotions unfold within it.

Yet it is not identical to any of them.

In many contemplative traditions this distinction is recognised in slightly different languages. Zen masters sometimes refer to the "original face" – not a literal face, but the awareness that exists prior to the stories we tell about ourselves. In Advaita Vedanta it is described as the witnessing consciousness that remains unchanged while thoughts and experiences come and go.

Understood in this light, Krishna's teaching does not describe an immortal personal identity moving from body to body. Rather, it points toward the recognition that the essence of our experience is not the constructed personality but the awareness within which that personality appears.

This interpretation aligns with a deeper philosophical insight shared across many traditions: what we take to be the "self" may be only a temporary formation within consciousness, not its owner.

The language of ancient scriptures can sometimes give the impression that a permanent individual soul travels intact through lifetimes. Yet the contemplative traditions that emerged from these teachings often emphasise something subtler – the discovery of a dimension of awareness that is not confined to the personal story we normally call "me."

Seen from this perspective, Krishna's message to Arjuna becomes less about preserving an individual soul and more about recognising the deeper ground of experience that remains unchanged even as the body and personality move through the changing circumstances of life.

Yet, while acknowledging this as a central belief and spiritual truth, many people translate it immediately into "my soul" – the notion that there is a permanent and pure entity residing somewhere inside the body. And yet, it is rarely encountered directly. People cannot point to it. They cannot locate it. They cannot clearly separate it from thought, feeling, memory, or personality. A subtle contradiction appears – almost unnoticed – and with it, a third figure enters.

The familiar body–soul duality becomes three distinct entities:

1. The body – visible, biological, mortal.
2. The soul – invisible, eternal, untouched.
3. The "me" – the egoic middleman who claims ownership of both.

This subtle triad – body, soul, and psychological 'me' – is rarely examined together. Each is spoken of separately. Each is defended passionately. But their coexistence generates contradictions that few are willing to confront.

And notice something subtle.

The body, in itself, is biology. It does not lament. It does not fear heaven or hell.

The soul, as described by scripture, is untouched, un–burnable, unchanging.

The only one who trembles is the psychological "me."
The one who claims ownership of the body.
The one who claims inheritance of the soul.

A middleman without title deeds.

It also creates a crisis at the moment of death. We are told the soul "Departs," but taken literally this becomes a category error. If the soul is eternal and omnipresent, its "departure" from the body would be like the ocean attempting to leave a single wave.

It has nowhere to go.
It is already everywhere the wave appears.

To travel to heaven or hell requires movement through space–time, a beginning and an endpoint, and a framework of conditions – karmic or moral – that can be applied to an individual. But an eternal entity does not move. It simply is. It cannot be judged, because it cannot be defiled. It cannot be rewarded, because it lacks nothing.

So, what actually departs at the time of death – and to where?

A student asked a sage, "When a lamp is extinguished, where does the flame go?"

The sage replied, "Show me where it came from."

Krishna – like many other masters, scriptures, and traditions – describes the Self as never born, never dying, never ceasing to be, and incapable of destruction. That is not the everyday "me" that lives a human life. The "me" is driven by thoughts, emotions, desires, cravings, attachments, and thought–based perceptions – ideas, concepts, and imaginations. Even if a soul exists, the ego does not ordinarily know it. The ego knows only its own narrative.

And conventional theology rarely abandons the soul, because without it the familiar architecture collapses: judgement, reward, punishment, heaven, hell. Yet under scrutiny, the question returns with force: what is it that leaves the body at death?

The contradiction becomes unavoidable. If it is "me" living this life – making decisions, carrying intentions, pursuing ambitions, accumulating "good" and "bad" outcomes – then is it "me" that departs when the body dies? But if it is the soul that departs, then the soul was never involved in my deeds in the first place. Why would it go anywhere? Krishna says it does not. It is eternal.

Then what becomes of heaven and hell? Or any other destination for that matter?

We will need to go deeper. It can only be one or the other. It could also be something else altogether.

If the soul dissolves under scrutiny, we are left with the body.

But what exactly is this body we so confidently identify with?

Is it solid?
Is it stable?
Is it truly "ours"?

Or is the body itself another kind of appearance – a structured event within deeper fields of reality?

The Buddha rejected the notion of a permanent soul, and yet he spoke of rebirth and the cycle of becoming. So, the question shifts again: if there is no enduring entity, what continues? What flows? What is carried forward – if not a "me," and not a personal soul?

If the soul dissolves under scrutiny, we are left with the body.

So, let's look at it carefully.

What exactly is this body we so confidently call "mine"? What is this structure we defend, nourish, decorate, protect, fear losing?

At first glance, the answer seems obvious. Flesh. Blood. Bone. Skin. A biological organism. A marvel of evolution.

But we have already walked through physics. We have already dismantled solidity once. We cannot now retreat into comfortable assumptions.

The body, as physics understands it, is not solid.

Every atom in this body is mostly empty space. The nucleus, dense but unimaginably small, sits at the centre like a grain of sand in a vast cathedral. The electrons are not tiny spheres orbiting like planets. They are probability distributions – clouds of likelihood, regions where something might be detected if measured.

What we call "touch" is not contact between solid objects. It is electromagnetic repulsion between fields. The sensation of solidity is resistance – structured interaction between charged particles.

The body, therefore, is not a thing. It is a field–structure.

And if we go deeper still, particles themselves are not little bits of substance. Modern quantum field theory tells us that what we call a particle is an excitation of an underlying field. An electron is not a standalone object. It is a localised vibration in the electron field. A photon is an excitation of the electromagnetic field.

The body is a pattern of vibrating fields.

Not metaphorically. Literally.

The body you defend so fiercely, the body you believe contains "you," is a dynamic configuration of energy patterns within quantum fields. It has no hard boundary in the way intuition imagines. The atoms composing it are not static possessions. They are exchanges. With every breath, you inhale atoms that were once elsewhere. With every exhale, you release atoms that become part of the world.

The boundary between "inside" and "outside" is functional, not absolute.

Now consider time.

Cells die. Cells regenerate. Molecules break apart and reform. The skin you touch today is not the same skin you had years ago. Blood renews. Bones remodel slowly over time. Proteins assemble and disassemble in continuous cycles.

The body is not a fixed structure. It is metabolic flux.

Even without invoking quantum mechanics, biology alone tells us the body is process, not object.

And yet we say: "This is me."

But which part?

One of the most striking illustrations of non–self appears in the ancient Buddhist dialogue known as The Questions of King Milinda.

In this dialogue, the monk Nāgasena is asked by the king to explain what a "person" really is.

Nāgasena responds with a question of his own.

He asks the king to describe the royal chariot that brought him to the monastery.

Is the chariot the wheels?
Is it the axle?
Is it the frame?
Is it the yoke or the reins?

The king replies that none of these individual parts alone constitute the chariot.

The chariot exists only as a convenient designation for the collection of parts assembled together.

Nāgasena then explains that the same is true of what we call a person.

The body is not the self.
Sensations are not the self.
Thoughts are not the self.
Memories are not the self.

What we call a person is simply a name given to the temporary combination of these processes.

When the conditions that hold these processes together change, the apparent entity we call a "self" dissolves – just as a chariot ceases to exist when its parts are disassembled.

Yet the causal processes that produced those conditions continue to unfold.

The carbon atom in your fingertip today was once in soil, in air, in another organism, perhaps in the body of someone long gone. It carries no memory of ownership. It has no loyalty to identity.

Physics insists on conservation. Energy is not created or destroyed. Matter transforms. Information reorganises.

Nothing disappears.

So, what is death, physically?

What ends is not substance, but coordination. The atoms remain. What ceases is their cooperation in sustaining a living pattern. The organisation dissolves. But the constituents remain. The atoms disperse into other forms.

The energy redistributes.

The universe does not lose anything.
It rearranges.
But let us go deeper still.

At the quantum level, the body is not even stable between moments in the way classical intuition assumes. Quantum fluctuations occur constantly. Virtual particles flicker into and out of existence within the vacuum. The fields themselves are restless.

What appears continuous is underwritten by discontinuity.
What appears solid is underwritten by probability.
What appears persistent is underwritten by constant renewal.

And here we must be careful.

Some interpretations of quantum mechanics suggest that measurement plays a role in the transition from possibility to actuality. Whether consciousness is required for this transition remains debated. The physics is not settled.

But this much is undeniable: at the foundational level, reality is not fixed substance. It is dynamic potential structured into temporary form.

The body, then, is not a container in which a soul resides. It is an event. A stabilised pattern within deeper, fluctuating fields. An eddy in a vast ocean of interaction.

Now return to the triad we exposed earlier:

Body
Soul
"Me"

If the soul is described as eternal, unchanging, untouched – it cannot be identical to this dynamic quantum flux.

There is a quiet irony here.

Theology stabilises the soul to make us feel secure. Physics destabilises the body to show us nothing is fixed.

In making the soul absolutely changeless, we may have rendered it incompatible with the living, breathing dynamism of reality itself.

It becomes a static ghost in a universe that never stands still.

If the body is a temporary configuration of fields – it cannot be a permanent self.

And if the "me" is a construct of thought, emerging from neural processes within this fluctuating biological pattern – then the entire structure of identity rests upon process, not substance.

There is no static entity anywhere in this chain.

Not in the body.
Not in the brain.
Not in the quantum field.

Only structured becoming.

And yet, experience is undeniably present. There is something it is like to be this configuration.

There is awareness of sensation. Awareness of thought. Awareness of this reading. But is that awareness located inside the body? Or is the body itself an appearance within awareness?

We must be careful not to leap prematurely into mysticism. The body exists. It bleeds. It ages. It feels pain. It requires food and oxygen. It obeys thermodynamic law. But its mode of existence is not what intuition assumes.

It is not a self–contained object moving through empty space. It is a dynamic participation in a relational universe.

The atoms composing it are older than humanity. Many were forged in stars billions of years ago. Stellar furnaces created the carbon backbone of life. Supernova explosions scattered heavier elements across galaxies.

The body is literally star–born matter temporarily organised into biological complexity.

There is no metaphysical poetry in that statement. It is astrophysical fact. And yet, when this arrangement dissolves, when the metabolic coordination ceases, when the neural firing stops – we say, "He is gone." "She has left."

Left where?

The atoms remain.
The energy remains.
The fields remain.
The quantum laws remain.

What has changed is pattern.

So now we confront something unsettling.

If the body is process, and the soul – as traditionally defined – cannot coherently interact with quantum matter without violating conservation or coherence, and the "me" is a cognitive construct dependent on neural patterning, then what exactly dies?

The event ceases.
The configuration ends.

But nothing substantial travels.
Nothing departs.

There is no object that exits the body in detectable form.
The universe does not release a hidden particle labelled "self."
The question itself may be mis–formed.

What ceases at death may not be a thing leaving, but a story no longer being told.

The narrative of "me" falls silent.
The biological coordination dissolves.
The pattern no longer sustains itself.

But nothing travels.

Instead of asking, "What leaves the body at death?" we might ask, "What was ever there as a separate entity to begin with?"

The body was always an arrangement. The "I" was always a narrative overlay. The soul, as eternal and untouched, could never have been entangled in biological drama in the first place.

And here we stand.

Not nihilism.
Not material reductionism.

But something more radical:

The body is not a prison for a soul.
It is a temporary stabilisation of universal process.

And whatever we truly are – if we are to speak carefully – cannot be located as a discrete object inside this flux.

We have dissolved solidity.
We have dissolved permanence.
We have dissolved ownership.
What remains is experience.
We have stripped the stage of its actors and its props.

The body, we found, was never a solid vessel but a shimmering, quantum event–a temporary stabilisation of universal fields.

One of the most common questions raised in Buddhist philosophy concerns rebirth.

If there is no permanent self, no soul that continues unchanged from one life to another, then what exactly is reborn?

At first glance the question seems to expose a contradiction. If nothing persists as a stable identity, how can the chain of rebirth continue? And if no enduring self exists, how can the law of – operate?

These questions were raised repeatedly during the Buddha's lifetime. His responses did not describe rebirth as the migration of a fixed soul from one body to another. Instead, he explained it as a process of continuity – a causal unfolding of conditions.

To illustrate this idea, Buddhist teachers often used simple analogies.

One of the most well–known compares rebirth to the lighting of one candle from another.

When a second candle is lit from the flame of the first, the new flame clearly depends on the original one. Without the first flame, the second would not arise. Yet it would be incorrect to say that the two flames are identical.

The second flame is neither the same flame nor entirely different.
There is continuity without identity.

A wave rising in the ocean may appear separate for a moment. It has a beginning, a crest, and an end. Yet the wave is never separate from the ocean itself.

When the wave subsides, nothing has truly disappeared. The water remains.

Another example offered in Buddhist texts is the echo produced by a sound. When a voice calls out across a valley, the echo that returns arises from the original sound. The echo depends upon it and carries its pattern, yet it is not the same sound that was first spoken.

The relationship is one of causal transmission, not the movement of a substance.

Similarly, the Buddha sometimes described rebirth in terms of a seed giving rise to a plant. The plant emerges from the seed and carries its genetic pattern, yet it is not identical to the seed itself. The seed dissolves in the process of becoming the plant.

These examples suggest that what continues from one moment to the next – and from one life to another in Buddhist thought – is not a soul or a fixed personal identity, but a stream of causes and conditions.

Thoughts condition future thoughts.
Actions condition future circumstances.
Intentions leave traces that influence the unfolding of experience.

This continuity of causation is what the Buddhist tradition refers to as –.
Karma, in this sense, does not require a permanent self that owns actions and carries them forward through time. Instead, it describes how actions and intentions shape the future through the natural unfolding of cause and effect.

Just as a ripple spreading across water continues to influence the movement of the surface long after the initial disturbance has passed, the effects of actions propagate through the unfolding process of existence.

Few ideas in spiritual traditions are as widely misunderstood as karma.
In popular imagination – is often portrayed as a cosmic reward and punishment system: good deeds earn reward, bad deeds invite punishment, and a soul carries the balance of these deeds from one life to another.

This interpretation, though widespread, does not fully reflect the deeper philosophical explanation found in early Buddhist teachings. In the Buddha's discourses, – is not primarily described as a moral ledger attached to a permanent self. Instead, it is explained as part of a much broader principle of causation – the natural unfolding of conditions through time.

Every intention, action, and mental state influences what arises next.

A thought conditions another thought.
An intention shapes behaviour.
A habit reinforces future tendencies.

Over time these patterns accumulate and interact, shaping the stream of experience that unfolds through life.

In this sense – is not a possession carried by an individual soul. It is the continuation of causal processes.

To understand this more clearly, Buddhist teachers often turned to simple images drawn from everyday life.

One of the most well–known compares rebirth to the lighting of one candle from another. When a second candle is lit from the first, the flame clearly arises because of the original flame. Without the first, the second would not appear.

Yet the new flame is not the same flame.

The relationship is one of continuity rather than identity.

Karma operates in a similar way. Actions and intentions generate consequences that condition future events, even though no fixed entity moves unchanged from one moment to the next.

Another traditional analogy compares existence to a flowing river. A river appears stable enough to be given a name and recognised as a single thing. Yet the water within it is constantly changing. No single drop remains.

The river continues through movement rather than permanence.

In much the same way, the unfolding of life continues through a chain of causes and conditions rather than through the persistence of a permanent self.

A story sometimes told by Buddhist teachers illustrates this idea in a simple way.

A traveller once walked through a valley and planted several seeds in the soil before continuing his journey. Years later another traveller passed through the same valley and found a flourishing orchard of fruit trees.

The second traveller enjoyed the shade of the trees and ate their fruit.

But the person who planted the seeds was no longer there.

Was the orchard created by the same person who now enjoys its fruits?

In one sense, no. The traveller who planted the seeds and the traveller who later rested under the trees were two different individuals.

And yet the orchard existed only because the seeds had once been planted.

The act and its consequence were separated by time, but the causal connection remained.

Karma works in a similar manner. Actions generate conditions that continue to influence the unfolding of events long after the original moment has passed.

But the consequences do not belong to a permanent self.

They belong to the process of causation itself.
At this point a deeper philosophical question emerges.

If there is no enduring self – no fixed individual who remains the same from moment to moment – then who experiences karma?

This question has been raised in many traditions.

Buddhism answers it by pointing out that the assumption behind the question may itself be mistaken. Karma does not require a permanent entity that owns actions and carries their results forward.

Instead, it describes how actions condition future events within a stream of experience.

Later non–dual teachers expressed this insight in even more direct terms.

The Indian sage Nisargadatta Maharaj often remarked that karma belongs only to the imagined person – the identity constructed from memories, habits, and beliefs about oneself. As long as we assume the existence of a personal doer, actions appear to accumulate as personal karma.

But when the nature of the self is examined deeply, the doer itself becomes difficult to locate.
Ramana Maharshi offered a similar line of enquiry. Rather than

explaining karma as something carried by an individual soul, he encouraged seekers to investigate the one who claims to act.

"Find out who the doer is," he would say.

When the sense of a separate doer dissolves under careful examination, the entire framework through which karma is normally understood begins to change.

Actions still occur. Consequences still arise. Cause and effect continue to operate throughout the unfolding of life.

But the idea of a fixed individual who owns those actions becomes increasingly difficult to sustain. Seen from this perspective, karma is neither a system of divine judgement nor a mechanism through which a permanent soul carries moral debts across lifetimes.

It is the unfolding of causation within a vast network of conditions.

Thoughts influence future thoughts.
Actions influence future circumstances.
Intentions shape the tendencies of the mind.

These influences may extend far beyond a single moment or even a single lifetime.

But what continues is not a person.

It is the movement of conditions giving rise to new conditions.

In Buddhist philosophy this unfolding is sometimes described as the stream of becoming.

Within that stream, what we call a "person" is a temporary pattern – much like a whirlpool that forms in a flowing river. The whirlpool appears stable for a time, yet the water that composes it is constantly changing.

In the same way, the identity we call "self" is a dynamic configuration of memories, perceptions, and habits arising within an ongoing process.

When the conditions sustaining that configuration dissolve, the pattern changes – but the flow of causation continues.

Understanding karma in this way shifts the focus of enquiry.

The Buddha repeatedly emphasised that intention lies at the heart of karma. "*It is intention, monks, that I call karma.*" A thought of anger, greed, fear, or compassion does not vanish when the moment passes. It leaves an imprint. Like a seed dropped into fertile ground, it conditions future thoughts, future choices, and future states of consciousness. Over time these countless seeds interact with one another, with other people, and with the circumstances of life, creating an intricate web of cause and effect far too complex to trace in a straight line.

Although the doctrine of karma is most strongly associated with Buddhist and Hindu traditions, reflections on moral causation and continuity across existence appear in many cultures.

The early Upanishads of India spoke of how actions shape the conditions of future life, declaring that a person becomes what they act and intend. Jain philosophers developed elaborate explanations of karmic influence, describing how actions leave subtle traces that shape future experience.

In ancient Greece, Pythagoras and later Plato entertained the idea that the circumstances of life are influenced by the ethical character formed in previous existences. Plato's Myth of Er portrays souls choosing future lives shaped by the tendencies they cultivated before. Stoic philosophers such as Marcus Aurelius described the universe as governed by an unbroken chain of causation in which every event unfolds from prior conditions within a rational cosmic order.

In Christian history, the early theologian Origen speculated that the circumstances of human life arise from conditions established before birth, though such ideas were later set aside by orthodox doctrine. Mystical traditions also expressed similar intuitions through poetic language.

The Sufi poet Rumi described existence as a continuous transformation through stages of being, suggesting that life unfolds through a long process of becoming rather than through fixed identities. Even in modern scientific thought, echoes of this insight appear in discussions of causality, systems theory, and behavioural conditioning.

Across cultures and centuries, thinkers have repeatedly recognised that human actions do not vanish without consequence. Instead, they participate in a vast unfolding network of causes and conditions shaping the patterns of existence.

Whether described as karma, fate, divine justice, or natural causation, many traditions have recognised a similar principle: actions shape the unfolding of life through chains of cause and effect.

Yet the deeper philosophical question remains unresolved.

If actions and consequences unfold within a vast network of conditions, who or what is the one that acts?

And if the self we believe ourselves to be cannot ultimately be found, then what is the nature of the awareness within which this entire process is experienced?

Through these enquiries, instead of asking how a permanent self carries actions through time, we begin to examine the nature of the processes unfolding within experience.

Life becomes less like a story owned by a central character and more like a vast web of interconnected events shaping one another.

And from within that unfolding, another question quietly emerges.
If the self is not a fixed entity, and if karma belongs to the movement of causes and conditions rather than to a personal soul, then what exactly is the awareness within which all of this is experienced?

This question brings us to the final stage of our exploration.

The ancient sages sometimes expressed this insight in a paradox:

As long as you believe you are the doer, – appears real and binding. When the illusion of the doer dissolves, the chain of ownership breaks.
Actions continue. Life continues. Cause and effect continue.

But the imagined centre that claims possession of them is no longer found. Seen in this light, rebirth is not the travel of a personal soul from body to body.

It is the continuation of a dynamic process.
The illusion of a fixed self–arises within this process, much as a whirlpool

forms within flowing water. The whirlpool may appear stable for a time, yet it is never composed of the same water from one moment to the next.

In the same way, what we call a person is a temporary configuration within an ongoing stream of physical and mental events.

When the conditions that sustain that configuration change or dissolve, the pattern itself changes – but the causal process continues.

The Buddhist explanation therefore avoids both extremes. It does not claim that a permanent soul survives unchanged after death. Nor does it claim that existence simply ends without continuity.

Instead, it describes a middle path: a chain of causes and conditions unfolding through time, where continuity exists without a fixed entity that possesses it.

The 'me,' that frantic narrator of our lives, has been exposed as a cognitive fiction, a ghost story told by a brain that is itself in constant flux. And the soul, if it is to be truly eternal, has proven too vast to be the passenger we once imagined.

Yet, in the silence that follows this deconstruction, a single, stubborn fact remains. Something was present to witness the flux. Something is here, reading these words, aware of the cold logic and the dissolving boundaries.

If there is no 'me' to own it, and no 'soul' to contain it, what is this light of experience that remains when the house is empty? We must now turn our gaze away from the objects of our identity and look directly at the act of looking itself.

We must turn fully toward that.
Not the body.
Not the soul.
Not the concept of "I."
But the raw fact of awareness itself.

Because if there is any anchor in this unfolding enquiry, it must be there.

And we have not yet looked directly at it.

If the self is not a fixed entity but a temporary configuration within an ongoing process of life, a deeper question naturally arises.

Throughout this entire unfolding – the body changing, thoughts appearing and disappearing, identities forming and dissolving – something seems to remain present.

Experiences are known.

Thoughts are observed.

Sensations are felt.

If I am not a body;
If I am not a soul;
If I am not who I think I am; then
Who am I?

Why am I?"

Who goes?
Who is reborn?

Why?

The mystery that now confronts us is therefore not the survival of a self, but the nature of the awareness within which all experience occurs.

PART III: THE COLLAPSE OF SEEKING

In the two parts that preceded this one, the enquiry began with the physical world - light, matter, time, space - and observed that none of these behave quite as ordinary perception suggests. It then turned to the mind that perceives them, tracing how the sense of self is assembled from sensation, memory, thought, and the movement of conditions rather than from any fixed, discoverable entity. Both lines of investigation converged on the same edge: the world we take for granted is not as solid as it appears, and the "I" we take ourselves to be is not as stable as it feels. What has not yet been examined directly is the awareness itself - the simple fact that something is present to notice all of this. This does not refer to another object hidden somewhere within experience, nor to the thoughts that describe it, but to the immediate fact of knowing itself - that by virtue of which sensations are felt, thoughts are known, and the passing movements of mind are noticed at all. This is what some Zen masters refer to as the "true self," though the language differs across traditions and the meanings are not always identical. Some call it consciousness. Krishna speaks of ātman. Many think of it as soul. The Buddha resists such definitions, perhaps recognising how quickly thought converts the unknown into doctrine. That is where the enquiry now turns.

Spiritual traditions often define consciousness as the primary ground of existence, while Western philosophical thought has historically shifted from a metaphysical soul to a subjective experience which the modern science still struggles to explain.

Contemporary philosopher David Chalmers attempted to distinguish between the "easy problems" (how the brain processes data) and the "Hard Problem" of consciousness. He defines consciousness as Qualia – the raw, subjective "what it is like" to see red or feel pain – which he argues cannot be explained by physical brain facts alone.

Masters like Adi Shankaracharya define consciousness (Chit) as the eternal, unchanging "witness" (Sakshi) to all experience. It is compared to a cinema screen: while movies (thoughts and world events) play upon it, the screen itself remains unaffected and is the only "true" reality.

Unlike Vedanta, many Buddhist schools (especially the Chittamatra or "Mind–Only"/Wu-Nian schools) see consciousness not as a fixed entity but as a "river"– a continuous flow of discrete moments of awareness. There is no permanent "self" behind the curtain; the "happening" of awareness is all there is.

In Sankhya and Yoga, consciousness is Purusha (the Seer), which is distinct from Prakriti (Nature/Matter). Evolution occurs so that the Seer can eventually recognise its own independence from the material world.

Across both Western and Eastern traditions, consciousness has usually been approached in one of five ways:

First, as the fact of experience itself – the simple "there is something it is like" to see, hear, feel, think, or be aware. Contemporary philosophy still treats this as the central puzzle. The Stanford Encyclopedia calls consciousness "perhaps no aspect of mind … more familiar or more puzzling," while the "hard problem" asks why any physical process should be accompanied by felt experience at all.

Second, as self–awareness or inner subjectivity – not merely awareness of the world, but awareness of oneself as the one to whom experience appears. Western philosophy has long examined this through self–consciousness, introspection, and the structure of subjectivity.

Third, as a process rather than a thing. William James described consciousness as a "stream," not a fixed substance, and many contemporary theories treat consciousness as arising from dynamic organisation, representation, or integration rather than from a soul–like entity. Higher–order theories, representational theories, and integrated information theory are all attempts to explain how conscious states arise from structured processes.

Fourth, as a function of the brain. Contemporary neuroscience holds that conscious experience depends on brain activity and seeks neural correlates and explanatory models for awareness, attention, reportability, and subjective access. This is the dominant scientific stance today, even though the explanatory gap remains open.

Fifth, as something more fundamental than the empirical person. This is where many Eastern traditions, and some Western philosophers and physicists, diverge from mainstream neuroscience. Rather than treating consciousness as a by-product of brain matter, they see it as primary and pervasive - not something the person possesses or the brain creates, but something in which the person appears. Human existence, in this view, is not the source of consciousness but one of the forms through which consciousness manifests itself. What we call personal awareness is therefore not an isolated creation of the ego, but a local expression of a deeper field of being.

In the Western tradition, Descartes famously grounded certainty in conscious thought – *cogito, ergo sum* – taking consciousness as the one indubitable fact. Kant later argued that experience requires a unifying structure of apperception, while phenomenology, from Husserl onward, turned to the careful description of lived experience itself. Existential and phenomenological thinkers then deepened this by asking how consciousness relates to time, selfhood, embodiment, and freedom.

Modern analytic philosophy reframed the issue. Consciousness became not only a metaphysical problem but also a conceptual one: what makes a state conscious? Is it representational content, higher–order awareness, integrated information, global prevalence, or some irreducible qualitative feature? The field remains plural and unresolved.

At the same time, Western neuroscience has become increasingly precise about what consciousness depends on. Brain damage, anaesthesia, sleep states, attentional modulation, and sensory integration all show that conscious experience is tightly linked to neural organisation. But even the best neuroscience still does not explain why neural activity should be accompanied by subjectivity at all. If we transplant an entire brain of one person into another, will their personalities switch? That is exactly why the "hard problem" remains so influential.

A more radical minority current in the West has kept open the possibility that consciousness is more basic than matter alone. Quantum approaches ask whether the strange indeterminacy at the foundation of physics leaves room for consciousness to play a deeper role than standard materialism allows. Panpsychism suggests that experience is not born suddenly in brains out of complete deadness, but is instead present in rudimentary form throughout reality, becoming organised in more complex ways in living beings. Dual-aspect views propose that mind and matter are not two separate worlds, but two faces of a deeper underlying ground. All of these remain controversial. They are difficult to test, easy to overstate, and none has produced a final or widely accepted solution. Yet their continued return is telling. It suggests that the question of consciousness has not been settled by reductionism but only contained by it for a time.

Modern neuroscience has made remarkable progress in understanding the brain. Researchers can observe neurons firing, map networks of neural activity, and identify regions of the brain associated with perception, memory, emotion, and decision–making.

We now know that the brain contains roughly *86 billion* neurons connected through trillions of synaptic pathways. Electrical impulses travel through these networks, chemical signals pass between cells, and complex patterns of activity emerge across the brain's architecture.

These processes are intimately linked with our experiences.

Damage to particular brain regions can alter perception, memory, or personality. Certain neural patterns correlate with attention, sleep, dreaming, or emotional states. Brain imaging technologies allow scientists to observe the dynamic activity underlying thought and behaviour.

Yet within all this detailed knowledge, one fundamental question remains unanswered.

How does physical activity in the brain give rise to subjective experience?

Why should the movement of electrical signals through networks of neurons produce the feeling of seeing a colour, hearing music, or experiencing joy and sorrow? This puzzle is that the contemporary philosophy describes as Chalmers' hard problem of consciousness.

The "easy problems" of neuroscience on the other hand explains how the brain processes information, controls behaviour, or integrates sensory inputs. These questions are difficult but appear solvable through scientific investigation.

The hard problem is different. It concerns the very existence of experience itself.

No matter how precisely we map neural activity, the transition from physical processes to conscious awareness remains unexplained.

A neuroscientist may observe patterns of electrical signals in the visual cortex when a person looks at a red flower. But the observation of neural activity does not explain why the experience of redness arises at all.

Some philosophers have compared this gap to attempting to explain the warmth of fire solely by describing the motion of molecules.

The description may be accurate, but it does not capture the felt quality of the experience.

Consciousness possesses a quality that scientists often describe as subjective experience.

There is something it is like to see a sunset.
Something it is like to hear a melody.
Something it is like to feel joy, sadness, or curiosity.

These experiences exist only from the first–person perspective.

They cannot be observed directly from the outside.

A brain scan may reveal neural activity correlated with the experience of pain, but the scan itself does not contain the pain. The subjective experience exists only for the person undergoing it.

This raises a profound philosophical question.

If consciousness arises entirely from physical processes, why does experience exist at all?

Why does the universe contain awareness?

Modern science generally approaches consciousness through a straightforward assumption: consciousness is produced by the brain.

According to this view, subjective experience arises from the activity of neural networks interacting through electrical and chemical signals. When neurons fire in particular patterns, perception, thought, and awareness emerge as properties of these physical processes.

From this perspective the brain is often compared to a sophisticated information–processing system. Just as software runs on the hardware of a computer, consciousness is thought to arise from the biological machinery of the brain.

Many contemporary theories of consciousness attempt to explain exactly how this might occur.

One prominent approach suggests that consciousness arises when information becomes highly integrated within neural systems. According to this theory, the brain generates consciousness because it forms an extraordinarily complex network in which information is continuously processed and integrated across many interacting regions. When neural activity reaches a certain level of complexity and interconnectedness, conscious experience emerges.

This approach attempts to explain consciousness as an emergent property – something that arises when physical systems become sufficiently organised.

Yet while such theories describe correlations between neural activity and experience, they still leave a fundamental question unanswered.

Why should information processing produce subjective experience at all?

A different proposal comes from physicist Roger Penrose and anaesthesiologist Stuart Hameroff, who have suggested that consciousness may involve quantum processes occurring within microscopic structures inside brain cells known as microtubules. Their theory, called Orchestrated Objective Reduction (Orch–OR), proposes that certain quantum events within these structures may contribute to the emergence of conscious awareness.

Hameroff proposed that microtubules within neurons might support quantum coherence long enough to influence neural processing. Coherence, in this context, refers to a state in which a system can exist in multiple possibilities simultaneously – often described, in simplified terms, as being in more than one state at once. Much like synchronised water waves that can amplify or cancel each other, coherent quantum states can interact to produce structured and predictable patterns.

This line of thinking opens an intriguing possibility: that aspects of consciousness may be closely linked to processes within the brain at a very fundamental level. At the same time, it also raises deeper questions. If consciousness arises from neural activity, does it remain entirely dependent on the brain, or is the brain participating in something more fundamental that it does not fully generate?

This question has long been explored in Western science and philosophy. Some approaches tend to view consciousness as an emergent property of complex biological systems, while others have suggested that it may not be fully reducible to physical processes alone. The enquiry, therefore, remains open. Rather than resolving the question of the self, it invites us to look more carefully at what we mean by identity, experience, and the sense of an inner "observer" that appears to inhabit the body.

Penrose argued that classical computational processes alone may not be sufficient to explain consciousness. He speculated that deeper physical processes – possibly related to quantum gravity – could play a role in generating conscious experience.

Even if we were to accept such a theory at face value, another question naturally follows: *what does this understanding change in the lived experience of a human being?* Does it alter how we perceive ourselves, or how we relate to the world?

In many cases, such knowledge remains at the level of intellectual insight. It becomes another piece of information the mind holds – something to think about, analyse, or discuss – yet life itself continues much as before - same person, same thoughts, same ego, same problems. The patterns of thought, emotion, and identity remain largely unchanged.

This points to an important distinction. There is a difference between knowing something conceptually and realising something directly. Conceptual understanding can inform and expand our view, but it does not necessarily transform the structure of our experience.

In contrast, what is often described in contemplative or spiritual traditions is not merely an addition of knowledge, but a shift in perception itself – a transformation in how reality is experienced. It is not something accumulated by the thinking mind, but something that alters the very sense of self and the way life is encountered.

The Orch–OR theory remains controversial within the scientific community. Some researchers consider it speculative, while others view it as an intriguing attempt to connect consciousness with the fundamental laws of physics.

Regardless of whether this particular theory proves correct, it highlights an important point.

Even among leading scientists, the nature of consciousness remains deeply uncertain.

What neuroscience has demonstrated with great confidence is that brain activity correlates with conscious experience.

Damage to certain brain regions alters perception and memory. Changes in brain chemistry influence mood and awareness. When the brain enters deep sleep or is placed under anaesthesia, conscious experience fades or disappears.

These observations strongly suggest that the brain plays a crucial role in shaping conscious experience.

Yet correlation does not necessarily imply complete explanation.
A radio receiver provides a useful analogy.

When the circuitry of a radio is damaged, the music stops. This does not mean that the radio itself created the music. The device may simply be receiving and translating signals originating elsewhere.

Some philosophers and scientists have therefore suggested that the brain might function less like a generator of consciousness and more like an interface or filter through which consciousness manifests.

This idea remains speculative, but it highlights an important gap in our understanding.

Neuroscience has shown how brain processes relate to experience. It has not yet explained why experience exists at all.

If consciousness were entirely produced by the brain, we might expect to find a clear mechanism through which neural activity generates subjective experience.

Despite decades of research, such a mechanism remains elusive.

Interestingly, the question of observation also appears in modern physics.

In quantum mechanics, the act of measurement plays a peculiar role in determining the behaviour of physical systems. Experiments such as the famous double–slit experiment suggest that particles behave differently depending on whether or not their behaviour is observed.

Physicists continue to debate the meaning of these results, but one conclusion is clear: the relationship between the observer and the observed cannot be ignored.

Niels Bohr emphasised that in quantum theory, the observer is not entirely separate from the phenomenon being observed. Is consciousness the observer because of which the reality collapses?

Similarly, the physicist Erwin Schrödinger – one of the founders of quantum mechanics – was deeply interested in the nature of consciousness. Schrödinger wrote that *consciousness cannot easily be explained as a product of physical processes alone.*

While physics does not provide answers to the mystery of awareness, it reveals that the traditional picture of a purely objective universe independent of observation may be incomplete.

Throughout our lives we naturally assume that somewhere within us there exists a centre – an observer who experiences the world.

When we say I see, I hear, or I think, it seems obvious that there must be someone inside the mind performing these acts. Perception appears to require a perceiver. Thoughts appear to require a thinker.

Yet when we begin to examine this assumption carefully, the picture becomes far less clear.

Modern neuroscience has explored the brain in extraordinary detail.

Researchers can identify the networks involved in vision, memory, language, emotional processing, and decision–making. They can observe how different regions of the brain cooperate to generate the rich tapestry of human experience.

But nowhere within this intricate architecture do scientists find a central observer.

There is no inner control room where a miniature version of us sits watching the world through the senses.

Instead, perception appears to emerge from distributed processes across many interacting regions of the brain. Visual signals travel from the eyes to the visual cortex, where different neural circuits analyse colour, shape, motion, and depth. These signals are then integrated with memory and interpretation to produce the experience we call seeing.

At no point in this chain does an independent observer appear.

The brain does not present information to a hidden spectator.

Rather, the processes themselves constitute the experience.

Philosophers sometimes refer to the imagined observer inside the head as the *homunculus* – a little person who supposedly watches the movie of the world unfolding in the brain.

But this idea leads to an immediate problem.

If a tiny observer inside the brain is watching perceptions, then who observes the perceptions of that tiny observer?

Would there need to be yet another observer inside that one?

This leads to an infinite regress – an endless chain of observers observing observers.

The conclusion many philosophers and neuroscientists reach is simple.

There is no inner spectator.

The sense of being an observer arises from the coordinated activity of many processes working together.

Recent developments in neuroscience offer another perspective.

According to the theory of predictive processing, the brain does not simply receive information from the world. Instead, it constantly generates predictions about what it expects to perceive.

Incoming sensory signals are compared against these predictions, and the brain updates its internal models accordingly.

Perception therefore emerges from an ongoing interaction between expectation and sensory input.

In this framework, experience is not presented to an observer inside the brain. Experience is the result of the brain's continuous attempt to interpret and predict the world. This has led some thinkers to explore alternative possibilities.

Perhaps consciousness is an emergent property of extremely complex systems.

Perhaps it is a fundamental feature of the universe, much like space, time, or energy.

Or perhaps the relationship between brain and awareness is more subtle than either science or philosophy has yet understood.

At present, none of these possibilities can be confirmed with certainty.
What remains undeniable, however, is that consciousness is the one phenomenon through which every aspect of our existence is known. Without awareness, there would be no experience of the universe at all.

At this point an intriguing convergence appears.

Ancient contemplative traditions encouraged seekers to investigate the nature of awareness directly. Modern science, approaching the problem from a completely different direction, has discovered that consciousness remains one of the deepest unsolved mysteries of the natural world.

The Upanishadic sages asked:

What is the essence of the one who experiences?

Neuroscience asks:

How can subjective experience arise from physical processes?

Physics asks:

What role does observation play in the structure of reality?

These questions arise from different traditions, yet they converge upon the same profound mystery.

The existence of awareness itself.

This leads to a striking possibility.

What we call observation may not require an independent observer at all.

Perception may simply be what occurs when complex systems of brain, body, and environment interact.

Thoughts appear.
Sensations arise.
Emotions unfold.

But the separate entity who claims ownership of these experiences cannot be located.

The mind tells a story about an "I" who observes everything, yet when we look carefully for that centre, it dissolves into the very processes it was supposed to control.

And yet something remains undeniable.

Experiences are occurring.

Thoughts appear and disappear.
Sounds are heard.
Colours are seen.
Memories arise.

Even if the observer cannot be found as a separate entity, the fact of experience itself remains.

This paradox lies at the heart of the mystery of consciousness.

If there is no inner observer directing the process, then what exactly is awareness?

Is consciousness merely another process within the brain?

Or does awareness represent something more fundamental – the field within which all experiences appear?

These questions have occupied philosophers, scientists, and contemplatives for centuries.

At this point in our enquiry, a subtle danger appears.

After examining the body and discovering that it is a changing biological process, and after questioning the stability of the personal self, the mind naturally looks for something deeper that might serve as the true centre of experience.

Many people then arrive at a comforting conclusion.

If the body is not the self and the personality is only a narrative constructed by the mind, then perhaps the true self must be consciousness.

In this view, consciousness is imagined as a kind of inner entity – a subtle observer residing somewhere behind the mind, watching the flow of thoughts and sensations.

Yet when we examine this assumption carefully, the same difficulty appears again.

Where exactly is consciousness?

Is it located in the brain?

Neuroscience has explored the brain in extraordinary detail, mapping networks of neurons responsible for perception, memory, attention, and emotional processing. Scientists can observe electrical activity and chemical interactions throughout the brain's complex architecture.

But no single location has been found where consciousness resides as a distinct object.

There is no identifiable structure that corresponds to a central "awareness module."

Instead, conscious experience appears to arise from the dynamic interaction of many distributed processes.

Vision involves networks across the visual cortex.
Language engages multiple regions across the brain.
Emotions involve intricate interactions between cortical and subcortical systems.

The brain functions less like a machine controlled by a central operator and more like an orchestra in which many instruments contribute to a constantly evolving pattern.

Philosophers sometimes describe a common error in human thinking known as reification – the tendency to treat processes as though they were things.

For example, we speak of a storm as if it were an object moving through the sky. Yet a storm is not a thing; it is a pattern formed by the movement of air, temperature, moisture, and pressure interacting across the atmosphere.

Similarly, we refer to a whirlpool in a river as though it were a separate entity. In reality, the whirlpool exists only as a dynamic pattern within flowing water.

Consciousness may be something similar.

What we call consciousness may not be an object hidden somewhere within the brain or body. It may instead be the process through which experience unfolds.

Thoughts arise, perceptions occur, sensations appear, emotions move through awareness. The continuous interaction of brain, body, and environment generates the stream of experience we call consciousness.

The mistake occurs when we imagine that behind this stream there must exist a separate entity who owns it.

This insight can initially feel unsettling because it challenges one of our most deeply rooted assumptions – that experience must belong to someone.

Yet when we examine experience carefully, the owner remains difficult to locate.

A sound appears in awareness.

Before a thought arises saying I hear that sound, the hearing has already occurred.

A sensation appears in the body.

Before the mind constructs the narrative, I feel this, the sensation is already present.

Thoughts themselves arise spontaneously. One thought leads to another, often without deliberate control.

Even the thought "I" am thinking is simply another thought appearing within the stream.

The sense of a central owner therefore emerges after the fact, as part of the narrative the mind constructs to organise experience.

Seen in this light, consciousness begins to resemble a dynamic process rather than a stable entity.

It is the unfolding of experience itself.

Just as a flame exists only as the ongoing process of combustion, awareness may exist only as the continuous arising of perceptions, sensations, and thoughts within the living system of brain and body interacting with the world.

This does not make consciousness unreal.

On the contrary, experience is the most immediate reality we know.
But it suggests that consciousness may not belong to an independent self.

It may be the living process through which the universe becomes aware of itself in a particular moment of time.

The Upanishadic tradition often treats the deepest consciousness not as the personal ego but as the underlying reality itself. The great mahāvākya Tat Tvam Asi points toward the identity of the deepest self and ultimate reality, later articulated in Vedanta as the relation between ātman and Brahman. In that framework, the ordinary personality is not the deepest truth of the individual.

Buddhism takes a different but equally profound route. Rather than affirming an eternal self, it denies a permanent soul–like essence through anattā and analyses the person into five aggregates, one of which is consciousness. Consciousness in Buddhism is real as a conditioned process, but it is not an enduring self. Britannica's summaries of anattā and the skandhas reflect this classical Buddhist view: the individual is a changing composition of psycho–physical factors, and no permanent soul can be identified within them.

This makes Buddhism especially important for your book, because it offers perhaps the clearest classical distinction between experience and owner of experience. Awareness occurs, but no permanent experiencer is found. That insight is later deepened in Mahayana traditions through emptiness, dependent origination, and the deconstruction of inherent identity.

Chinese and Zen traditions then radicalise the experiential side of the enquiry. Instead of constructing metaphysical systems, they often point directly to awareness before conceptualisation – immediate, non–grasping, prior to self–image. Zen's emphasis is not on defining consciousness but on seeing through the mind's constructions. This is closely related to phenomenological and contemplative observation rather than doctrinal speculation. This connection is interpretive, but it fits the broader pattern of East Asian Buddhist thought grounded in anattā and emptiness.

Tibetan traditions, meanwhile, preserve a more elaborate analysis of consciousness across death, dream, meditation, and rebirth. Texts like the Bardo Thödol treat consciousness as traversing states, but again not as a Western–style immortal personality.

The deepest convergence is this:

both traditions recognise that the ordinary ego is not the whole story
both struggle to explain how subjective experience relates to the world
both repeatedly discover that consciousness cannot be treated as just

another object among objects

Western philosophy tends to ask: *How can consciousness be explained?*
Eastern traditions more often ask: *Who is the one that claims to be conscious?*
Modern neuroscience asks: *What brain processes correlate with conscious states?*
Buddhism asks: *Can a self be found within those processes?*
Vedanta asks: *What remains when all changing contents are negated?*

Across both Eastern and Western traditions, consciousness has remained the final mystery: in the West, because it resists reduction to matter; in the East, because it reveals that the one who claims ownership of experience cannot be found.

In early Buddhist Abhidhamma teachings, particularly preserved in the Theravāda tradition, the transition between lives is described as the arising of a new consciousness known as patisandhi–viññāṇa – the rebirth–linking consciousness.

One of the most misunderstood ideas in Buddhism is rebirth. When people hear that Buddhism teaches rebirth, they often imagine something similar to the Hindu notion of an immortal soul migrating from one body to another. But the Buddha repeatedly rejected the existence of such a permanent self.

If there is no enduring soul, then a natural question arises:

What exactly is reborn?

The Buddha's answer is subtle. Nothing permanent travels from one life to another. Yet the causal process that constitutes a life does not end with death. Instead, it continues.

This continuation is explained through the concept of rebirth consciousness.

At the moment when the body dies and the final consciousness of that life ceases; a new consciousness arises conditioned by the accumulated karmic tendencies of the previous life. This new consciousness does not carry a self, personality, or soul across the boundary of death. Rather, it carries causal momentum.

The Buddha compared this process to several simple but powerful images.

A flame lighting another flame.

The two flames are not the same flame, yet neither are they entirely different.

An echo following a sound. The echo depends on the original sound but is not the sound itself.

Or milk turning into curd, then butter, then ghee.

Each stage arises from the previous one, yet none is identical to the earlier form.

In the same way, the consciousness that arises at rebirth is neither the same as the previous consciousness nor completely unrelated to it.

It is continuity without identity.

This process is grounded in one of the central insights of Buddhist philosophy: dependent origination (pratītyasamutpāda).

The Buddha described existence not as a chain of fixed entities but as a network of conditions giving rise to one another. In the famous twelvefold chain, consciousness arises conditioned by karmic formations and in turn conditions the development of mind and body.

Ignorance conditions mental formations.
Mental formations condition consciousness.
Consciousness conditions name and form.
And the process unfolds into the entire structure of lived existence.

Thus, rebirth consciousness is not a mysterious soul entering a body. It is the continuation of causal conditioning within the stream of becoming.

In Buddhist thought this is sometimes called the stream of consciousness (viññāṇa–sota).

Like a river, it appears continuous. Yet the water flowing through it is never the same from moment to moment.

Karma in Buddhism is not divine judgment, moral bookkeeping, or cosmic reward and punishment. It is the law of intentional causation.

Every intentional action – physical, verbal, or mental – leaves a subtle imprint in the stream of consciousness. These imprints are not stored somewhere like files in a cabinet. Rather, they influence the tendencies and conditions that shape future experiences.

At the moment of death, these karmic potentials help determine the conditions under which rebirth consciousness arises.

This does not mean a personality transfers intact. The memories, language, social identity, and personal narrative associated with the previous life dissolve with the brain and body that sustained them.

What continues is more subtle:

Tendencies
Latent impressions
Karmic momentum
The unfolding of causes and conditions

Here lies the profound paradox that Buddhism invites us to contemplate.

If there is no enduring self, then who experiences the results of karma?

The Buddha answered this question by refusing to accept its premise.

He pointed out that the idea of a fixed experiencer is itself an illusion constructed from the five aggregates: body, sensations, perceptions, mental formations, and consciousness.

These aggregates are constantly changing processes. What we call a "person" is simply their temporary configuration.

Thus, the one who performs an action and the one who later experiences its consequences are neither identical nor entirely separate.

They are linked through causation.

To understand rebirth consciousness, the Buddha encouraged his followers to abandon the idea of a fixed entity travelling through time.

Instead, imagine a stream.

At every moment new water flows into it. Old water flows away. Yet the river appears continuous.

Similarly, what we call a person is a dynamic stream of physical and mental processes. Birth and death are not the beginning and end of a soul but transitions within this flow.

From this perspective, rebirth becomes less mysterious.

It is simply the continuation of causation.

This teaching carries a radical implication.

If the self is constructed moment by moment through perception, memory, and thought, then the identity we defend so fiercely may not exist in the way we imagine.

The Buddha's teaching on rebirth is therefore not merely about future lives.

It is about seeing, here and now, that the "I" we believe ourselves to be is already a continuously changing process.

The one who was here yesterday is not exactly the one who is here now.

And yet, through memory and narrative, we maintain the sense that they are the same.

Rebirth simply extends this principle beyond the boundary we call death.

This is where a new image begins to emerge: that consciousness may not be produced by the brain, but rather channelled through it. Just as a radio receiver captures waves that already exist in the atmosphere, the human nervous system may act as a tuning device for a field of awareness that is more fundamental than matter. The Buddha's rejection of a "self" does not necessarily imply nothingness; it could point to the idea that individuality is a temporary resonance in a larger field.

Quantum physics gives an eerie support to this metaphor. The double–slit experiment shows that particles behave as waves until observed, collapsing into form when measured. But who or what does the "observing"? If consciousness is not a late by–product of neural chemistry but the very factor that brings potentiality into actuality, then it is more primary than matter itself. This does not mean an eternal soul watching from behind the scenes; rather, it suggests that awareness is woven into the very fabric of the cosmos, a quality of existence as fundamental as space–time or energy.

As science continued to probe deeper into the nature of reality, a subtle shift began to emerge in how some of its most thoughtful contributors approached the question of consciousness. What began as a purely objective investigation into matter and energy gradually opened into something more nuanced – and, at times, more uncertain.

In the early development of quantum theory, figures like Max Planck began to recognise that the observer could not be entirely separated from what was being observed. Planck suggested that consciousness might not simply arise from matter but could be more fundamental to it.

This perspective found a different expression in the work of Niels Bohr. Bohr did not argue that consciousness creates reality, but he showed that the conditions under which we observe a system fundamentally shape what can be said about it. In his principle of complementarity, light and matter could behave as either waves or particles, depending on how they were measured. The reality we describe, therefore, is not entirely independent of the way we engage with it. It is not that the observer invents reality, but that observation defines the framework within which reality appears.

This line of enquiry deepened with Erwin Schrödinger, who reflected on consciousness not as something divided among individuals, but as a single underlying awareness appearing as many. Werner Heisenberg similarly showed that the act of measurement introduces fundamental limits to what can be known simultaneously, reinforcing the idea that reality is not a fixed, fully accessible structure.

Later, thinkers such as John Wheeler extended this into the notion of a participatory universe, where observers are not passive spectators but active participants in how reality unfolds. Even more recent perspectives, including those of Roger Penrose, continue to question whether consciousness can be fully explained within existing physical frameworks.

Across these perspectives, there is no single conclusion. Yet a pattern quietly emerges. As enquiry moves closer to the foundations of matter, the clear boundary between observer and observed begins to soften.

What once appeared as a separate world "out there" and a perceiving mind "in here" becomes less sharply defined.

Science does not resolve this into a final answer. Instead, it leaves us with a deeper question – one that is not confined to equations or experiments but reaches into the nature of experience itself.

A different kind of clarity emerges in the work of Richard Feynman, who approached quantum mechanics with both precision and humility. Feynman openly acknowledged that, despite its extraordinary predictive power, quantum theory resists intuitive understanding. Reflecting on experiments such as the double–slit, he famously remarked that no one truly "understands" quantum mechanics. Rather than forcing the theory into familiar mental models, he encouraged accepting its strangeness as a fundamental feature of nature. In doing so, he shifted the emphasis from explanation to observation – from trying to make reality conform to human intuition, to recognising that reality may not be obliged to align with it. His perspective leaves us with an important insight: the limits we encounter may not lie in the universe itself, but in the frameworks through which we attempt to comprehend it.

Neuroscience, meanwhile, has uncovered that perception and thought are not direct imprints of reality but reconstructions, dependent on brain structures constantly updating patterns from past experience. The "self" emerges as a narrative – a continuous editing of memory, sensation, and expectation. Strip away the narrative, as deep meditation sometimes allows, and one encounters pure awareness without story. In those moments, the brain no longer asserts its central role as narrator; it simply receives. This is why mystics describe states of vastness, light, or silence, where "I" disappears but awareness remains luminous.

In karmic terms, this model resolves a long–standing puzzle. If there is no self, what continues after death? Not an unchanging soul, but a transmission of patterns – a ripple of information within the field of awareness. Just as one candle lights another without transferring its substance, karmic tendencies pass into new configurations without any "self" being transported. The brain dies, but the informational coherence it carried does not vanish; it reorganises within the field, seeking resonance in new conditions. This is rebirth without a self, continuity without identity.

Ancient myths intuited this in symbolic language: the soul leaving the body, the spark of divine fire moving on, the gods breathing life into clay. Buddhism stripped away the metaphors and left only the mechanics of dependent origination. Quantum physics, still groping for language, speaks of entanglement, collapse, and non–locality. Neuroscience speaks of networks, plasticity, and emergent properties. All are different maps pointing toward the same mystery: consciousness is not merely inside us; it is the medium in which we exist.

And if that is true, then death is not an end but a change of frequency. The individual receiver stops functioning, but the field of awareness continues to vibrate. The challenge for us – as practitioners, scientists, or seekers – is not to prove this metaphysically but to experience, in our own stillness, how the "I" dissolves and yet awareness remains.

We have travelled through many layers of enquiry – from the workings of the brain to the strange behaviour of particles, from philosophical reflection to contemplative insight. Along the way, the certainty we once held about the nature of self and consciousness has gradually softened. What seemed obvious at the beginning – that there is a distinct "I" inside the body, thinking, choosing, and experiencing – now appears less clear, more elusive.

And yet, something remains.

Experience continues. Thoughts arise. Sensations are felt. Life unfolds. The body breathes, moves, ages. The world appears, moment by moment, with remarkable coherence. Whether we describe it in terms of neural activity, quantum processes, or streams of consciousness, the fact of experience itself does not disappear.

So, we are left standing at a threshold.

On one side lies explanation – models, theories, and interpretations that attempt to describe how consciousness might arise or function. On the other side lies something that cannot be fully captured in description alone: the immediacy of being, the directness of experience, the simple fact that there is awareness.

The question now begins to shift.

It is no longer only about what consciousness is, or where it comes from. It becomes a more intimate enquiry: what is it that is present before any explanation is formed? What remains when thought, identity, and interpretation are seen for what they are?

Perhaps this is where understanding, as knowledge, reaches its limit – and something else begins.

The next step, then, is not to add more theories, but to look more closely – not at the world as an object, but at experience itself. Not as an idea, but as it is lived.

And from there, we may begin to see what, if anything, is truly known.

We have questioned the world and found that it is not as solid as it appears. We have questioned time and found that the present is not universal. We have questioned perception and discovered that what we see is assembled within the mind. We have questioned the body and found it to be a temporary gathering of atoms, sensations, and memories. We have questioned the soul and found no certainty there either.

And then, quietly, the enquiry turned toward the one who was asking all these questions.

The one who seeks.

The one who wants meaning, certainty, permanence, and truth.

Yet the deeper we looked, the more difficult it became to find such a one. There were thoughts, emotions, memories, reactions, desires, fears, and images. There was the sense of being someone at the centre of experience. But there was no clear boundary where this "I" began, nor any fixed substance from which it was made.

Perhaps this is why the search becomes so exhausting. We imagine that there is someone who will eventually arrive somewhere - someone who will finally understand, attain, awaken, or become complete. But what if the seeker is itself part of what is being sought? What if the very movement of seeking keeps alive the sense that something is missing?

There comes a point in enquiry where no further answer satisfies. Not because the questions are wrong, but because every answer still belongs to thought, and thought cannot step outside itself to grasp what lies beyond it.

Then something unexpected becomes possible.

Not another conclusion.

Not another belief.

But a pause.

A stillness in which the compulsion to search begins to loosen.
What remains when the movement of seeking falls silent? What is here before thought names it, before memory compares it, before the mind turns it into a story?

The chapters that follow do not attempt to provide another philosophy. They move more quietly than what came before. They do not ask you to think harder, but perhaps to notice more deeply.

For once the seeker is no longer taken for granted, what remains is not emptiness in the ordinary sense. It is not a void, a denial, or an absence. It is simply an experience before it becomes "mine."

We now enter that silence.

PART IV: OPENING INTO SILENCE

Let's talk about life.

There comes a point where enquiry begins to turn.

Up to now, the questions have been directed outward – toward the universe, toward matter, toward time, toward the nature of consciousness. We have examined theories, explored paradoxes, and followed the edges of scientific and philosophical thought as far as they seem willing to go.

But something subtle begins to shift.

The search no longer feels satisfied with explanations alone.

No matter how refined the models become, or how elegant the theories appear, they remain descriptions – interpretations of reality, not reality itself. They organise thought, but they do not dissolve the one who is thinking.

And so, the direction of the enquiry changes.

It begins to turn inward – not in the sense of retreating from the world, but in the sense of looking more closely at the very field in which the world appears.

Not as an idea.
Not as a belief.
But as immediate experience.

This shift is not philosophical. It is experiential.

It does not ask, "What is consciousness?"

It asks, "What is present, right now, before that question even arises? And, who experiences it?"

This movement does not begin as a grand search for truth. It begins more quietly - as a sense that something fundamental is being overlooked. Life continues as it does for most of us: work, responsibilities, conversations, ambitions, moments of joy, and moments of strain. Yet beneath all of this lies a persistent feeling that what we take ourselves to be - this constant "I" at the centre of experience - is not as solid or as fixed as it appears.

At first, this starts as an intellectual curiosity.

But over time, it has the potential to become something else.

A question that could not be set aside.

If we continue to look at human life through the lens of biology, much can be explained with remarkable precision. Cells divide, tissues form, organs develop. Genetic instructions unfold with extraordinary complexity, guiding the formation of a living body from a single fertilised cell. Science has mapped these processes in great detail – from DNA replication to neural development – revealing a system of astonishing order and coherence.

And yet, something essential remains unaccounted for.

Biology can describe how biological structures form. It can explain how cells are formed and behave, how signals are transmitted, how neurons fire, how networks process information. But it does not fully explain the simple, undeniable fact that there is experience. That there is something it is like to be here – to see, to feel, to be aware.

A body can be described. A brain can be analysed. But the felt sense of being – the immediacy of experience – does not appear as an object within those descriptions.

Even at the very beginning of life, this question quietly arises. A fertilised embryo can be formed under controlled conditions. Cells can be observed dividing, differentiating, organising into increasingly complex structures. And yet, at what point does this become a lived experience? At what point does there arise not just biological activity, but the presence of awareness? When does the life itself enter?

Different traditions have approached this question in different ways. Some speak of a "soul" entering the body at a certain stage of development. Others describe a continuity of consciousness that finds new expression at conception. Still others avoid such definitions altogether, pointing instead to a process that cannot be easily captured in language.

Science, for its part, continues to explore the mechanisms of life with increasing sophistication. But the emergence of subjective experience – the fact that life is not only occurring but is being experienced – remains one of its deepest open questions.

And so, even within a fully functioning biological system, something remains unresolved.

The body can be alive. The brain can be active. Processes can be measured.

But the question persists:

Where does the sense of being arise?

As science continues to advance, our ability to understand and replicate aspects of life has grown remarkably. We can model intelligence, build machines that learn, simulate decision–making, and even manipulate the building blocks of biology. From artificial intelligence to genetic engineering, the boundaries of what can be constructed or replicated are expanding rapidly.

And yet, something about human experience still appears distinct.

If we follow the scientific view to its logical conclusion, consciousness may be seen as arising from sufficiently complex neural systems. In that case, any organism with a developed nervous system – animals, birds, even marine life – would, in some form, be generating its own field of experience.

This may well be true.

But even if we were to fully explain the mechanisms of consciousness, a deeper question remains. Would such an explanation transform the way we live? Or would it become, like many other discoveries, another layer of understanding added to the mind – informative, perhaps even fascinating, but leaving the structure of experience largely unchanged?

And then another question begins to surface.

If consciousness is present across many forms of life, what distinguishes human experience? Why does the question of meaning, self, and existence arise so intensely here? Why this persistent search – for truth, for liberation, for understanding?

In many contemplative traditions, particularly in the teachings of the Buddha, human life is regarded as uniquely poised. Not because it is inherently superior, but because it appears to hold a rare balance: the capacity to reflect, to question, and to observe experience itself. It is said that this balance – between instinct and awareness, between suffering and insight – creates the conditions in which deeper realisation becomes possible.

Other forms of life may experience, respond, and adapt with great sensitivity. But the ability to turn attention inward – to question the nature of the experiencer itself – seems, at least from our current understanding, to be most fully developed in the human condition.

And so, the question deepens.

If consciousness is not exclusive to humans, yet self-awareness seems to reach a particular intensity here, what is it that makes this form of life so significant?

Is it simply biological complexity?

Or is there something about human experience that allows a different kind of seeing – one that does not merely engage with the world, but begins to enquire into the very nature of reality itself?

As the enquiry deepens, it begins to move away from accumulation and toward a very different kind of seeing. Across cultures, across centuries, and across traditions, certain voices begin to converge on a strikingly simple insight: what we are seeking may not be something to be attained, but something to be recognised.

The very idea of a "journey" is gently questioned.

A journey assumes distance – something far away, something to be reached, and someone who must travel to get there. But what if this assumption itself is the subtle illusion?

In the teachings of Ramana Maharshi and Nisargadatta Maharaj, the enquiry is turned back upon the seeker. Rather than searching outward, one is invited to ask a simple but penetrating question: *Who am I?* Not as a philosophical exercise, but as a direct investigation. And in that enquiry, something unexpected begins to unfold. The one who is searching cannot be found as a solid entity. What remains is not an answer, but a quiet recognition – that the "I" assumed to be at the centre of experience may never have existed in the way it was imagined.

In Zen, this insight is expressed with uncompromising clarity. Huang Po taught that there is only One Mind, and that the search for a separate self is like using fire to look for fire. *The more one seeks, the more one reinforces the illusion of a seeker.* What is required, he suggests, is not effort in the usual sense, but the ending of conceptual thought – the dropping of the very structures that sustain the sense of separation.

A similar simplicity appears in Taoist thought. In the writings of Zhuangzi, the idea of wu wei (*wuwei*) – effortless action – points to a way of living in which there is no central controller managing life. Actions unfold naturally, as part of the larger movement of the Tao. The sense of a separate "doer" softens, and with it, the tension of control. One listens not through effort, but through openness – as if the self were not a solid centre, but a hollow space through which life moves.

In Sufi mysticism, this dissolution takes on a more devotional expression. The doctrine of unity, often described as Wahdat al–Wujud, speaks of the individual self as a veil over a deeper reality. Mansur Al–Hallaj, in his famous utterance "Ana al–Haqq" – I am the Truth – was not asserting personal identity but pointing to its absence. The individual had dissolved, leaving only the expression of the whole.

Even within Western contemplative traditions, echoes of this insight appear. Meister Eckhart spoke of a union so complete that the distinction between the soul and the divine disappears. "The eye with which I see God," he wrote, "is the same eye with which God sees me." To arrive at this, one must become empty – not only of possessions or ideas, but of the very sense of being a separate self.

More contemporary teachers have pointed in the same direction with striking directness. Douglas Harding invited a simple observation: from one's own immediate experience, there is no head, no centre – only an open field in which the world appears. Jean Klein similarly emphasised that what we take ourselves to be is largely a social and conceptual construct. What remains, when this is seen clearly, is not a person observing experience, but awareness itself – the listening, rather than the listener.

In the non–dual traditions of India, this understanding has been articulated in many forms. In Advaita Vedanta and Kashmir Shaivism, the sense of a separate doer is seen as an illusion arising within consciousness. The Bhagavad Gita speaks of actions being carried out by the forces of nature, while the individual, under the influence of ego, assumes ownership: "I am the doer." When this misidentification falls away, life continues – but without the burden of a separate controller.

Texts such as the Ribhu Gita take this insight to its furthest edge, declaring that there is no individual self, no separate mind – only the formless reality appearing as all forms. The Shiva Sutras begin with the simple assertion: consciousness itself is the Self. What obscures this is not distance, but misidentification – a subtle contraction into individuality.

Across these traditions, the language differs, the metaphors vary, the cultural expressions change.

But the gesture is the same.
Not toward becoming something new,
but toward seeing what has always been the case.

And perhaps this is where the enquiry takes its most unexpected turn.

If there is no separate "I" at the centre of experience,
then what is it that has been seeking all along?

And yet, this insight – that the "I" we take ourselves to be may not exist in the way we assume – does not sit easily with the mind.

Across cultures, whether in the West or the East, much of our thinking is quietly organised around a central reference point: a self that experiences, chooses, remembers, and continues. Nearly all our language, our systems of meaning, and our personal narratives are built upon this assumption. To imagine reality without this centre can feel not only unfamiliar, but almost inconceivable.

There is also something more subtle at play.

The very structure of thought seems to preserve this sense of identity. Even when exposed to ideas of awareness, soul, or consciousness, the mind often absorbs them in a familiar way – as something it possesses, something it can understand, attain, or become. The language may change, but the underlying assumption remains – that there is still a "someone" at the centre to whom all of this belongs.

In this way, the sense of self does not disappear easily. It adapts. It refines itself. It gathers new concepts, even spiritual and divine ones, and incorporates them into its own continuity.

And so, what is being pointed to in these teachings is not merely another idea to be accepted, but something far more radical – a seeing that does not confirm the self but quietly questions its very foundation.

Experience is the brain's-controlled hallucination of reality. It begins with transduction, where your sense organs convert raw physical energy–like light waves or air vibrations–into the "common currency" of electrical pulses. These pulses travel to specific processing hubs, like the visual cortex or thalamus, where the brain doesn't just "see" the world but actively constructs it.

The brain compares this incoming data against a massive library of prior expectations and memories. It ignores most of the noise and highlights what it deems important, creating a "best guess" of what is happening outside. This processed data is then integrated across the prefrontal cortex, where disparate signals of colour, sound, and emotion are woven together into a single, seamless subjective narrative–the feeling of "being here" in this moment.

So, what is it, without which even a fully functioning biological system does not become aware – and yet which is often spoken of as fundamental to existence? And how does it come to be?

We know that the body is composed of elements that are not unique to us. The atoms that form us have existed long before our birth and will continue long after the body dissolves. In accordance with the laws of nature, nothing is truly lost – it transforms, rearranges, and returns to the wider universe. From this perspective, the body is a temporary arrangement – a pattern formed out of conditions, sustained for a period of time, and eventually dispersed.

And yet, within this configuration, something appears that is not so easily described.

There is experience.
There is awareness.
There is a sense of being.

This has been recognised, in different ways, across cultures and traditions – not as a "thing" that can be located, but as something more fundamental to existence itself. It is not the constructed identity we call "I", nor is it easily reduced to a concept such as a "soul" in the conventional sense.

And yet, to define it directly proves difficult.

This extraordinary organ translates electrical and chemical activity into the seamless experience of a world – and, within it, the feeling of being a self.

And yet, even with all its complexity, a question remains.

Does the brain produce awareness?
Or does it organise, filter, and express something more fundamental?

The human brain, weighing roughly three pounds, contains approximately 86 billion neurons, each forming thousands of connections. The resulting network – with over 100 trillion synapses – is a dynamic, ever–changing system of electrical and chemical activity. Signals move through it at remarkable speeds, shaped by ionic gradients, neurotransmitters, and intricate feedback loops.

Through this activity, the brain performs an extraordinary function.

It converts light into vision, vibration into sound, chemical signals into taste and smell. It integrates these streams into a coherent world. More than that, it constructs a continuous narrative – a seamless sense of "being here," experiencing life as a unified flow.

Modern neuroscience often describes this as a form of controlled hallucination. The brain does not passively receive reality; it actively predicts, filters, and assembles it, drawing from memory and expectation to produce a "best guess" of what is happening.

Within this constructed experience, the feeling of a self also arises.

A centre appears – a sense of "I" who sees, thinks, chooses, and lives.

But when observed closely, this "I" does not seem to have an independent existence. It is not found in any specific neural structure. It emerges as part of the narrative itself – a functional construct that helps organise experience.

This raises a subtle but important question.

If the brain can construct the sense of a self, could it also be that what we call awareness is not something it produces, but something it organises?

There was once an unknown master in Mumbai, not too long ago – at least not long in the measure of a human life.

He had no formal education. He had never studied science in any conventional sense.

And yet, in the course of simple conversations, he would speak of the brain, of neurons and synapses, of patterns and decay – as though he had arrived there not through study, but through direct observation.

Someone once asked him:

"When I am asleep – when there are no thoughts, no images, no sense of the world – who is aware?"

He smiled, almost playfully.

"Who is asking this question?" he replied.
"Is it you?"

He did not answer.

Or perhaps, he refused to give one. Because to give an answer, he would say, is to give the mind something to hold.

"And whatever you are told," he would often say,
"you will turn into knowledge – and then into belief."

"And belief," he would add quietly, "is the end of enquiry."

So instead, he would return the question.

Not as a technique.
Not as a practice.
But as a simple redirection.

Find out who is seeking.
Not intellectually.
Not as an idea.

But directly.

At times, his observations moved into territories that seemed almost scientific in language, though he never claimed them as such.

He would say that what we take to be beings – higher, divine, or otherwise – may not exist as solid forms in the way we imagine. Rather, they may exist as patterns – as subtle fields, as vibrations – not unlike electromagnetic phenomena, though not reducible to them.

And when it comes to their appearance, he would suggest something even more disquieting: That what is seen is shaped not only by what is there, but by how it is received. If two people hold entirely different images of the same deity, and something were to appear – would they see the same form? Or would each see what their own mind is already prepared to see? Ultimately, he said, "it is the neurons" that give shape to the vibration.

The question lingers. Because it echoes something familiar. Remember the double–slit experiment? Copenhagen interpretation? Collapse of the wave function when observed? It is a strange parallel with the modern physics – where observation does not merely reveal reality but appears to participate in its formation. Where what is seen depends, in subtle ways, on how it is looked at.

But he never used such parallels. He never attempted to prove anything.

He simply pointed – again and again – to the same place:

Do not collect answers.
Do not accumulate conclusions.
Find out what is looking.
And remain there.

What if the brain is not the origin of consciousness, but its instrument?

At some point in this enquiry, a different way of looking begins to take shape.

Rather than seeing consciousness as something that enters the body, or is created within it, it becomes possible to consider that it may already be present – and that the brain functions as a medium through which it is expressed.

In this view, the body is not separate from consciousness, nor is it its source. It is a configuration – a temporary coherence within a much larger field.

A simple analogy may help.

A wave forms on the surface of the ocean. It has a beginning, a shape, a movement, and an apparent individuality. Yet, at no point is it separate from the ocean. Its existence depends entirely on underlying conditions – currents, wind, and depth. When those conditions change, the wave subsides.

Nothing has been lost. The form disappears, but the ocean remains.

Human life may be understood in a similar way.

There may be no separate entity that enters the body at birth or leaves it at death. Instead, what we call a life is a temporary pattern – a coherent organisation of processes through which experience arises.

When the conditions that sustain this pattern dissolve, the pattern ends. But that does not necessarily imply the disappearance of what underlies it. In many traditions, this continuity is described not as the survival of a person, but as the continuation of causal patterns – tendencies, impressions, and conditions unfolding over time.

This is often expressed through the language of karma and rebirth.

Here, rebirth does not require a fixed self that travels from one life to another. Rather, it suggests a continuity without identity – a process without a central owner.

A flame passing from one candle to another is not the same flame, and yet it is not entirely different.

In this sense, what continues is not "someone," but the unfolding of conditions.

And perhaps, within this unfolding, there exists the possibility – not of becoming something new, but of recognising what has always been present.

At some point, this enquiry stopped being a question to think about.

It did not arrive as an answer.
It did not resolve itself through logic.
It did not come from reading, or from assembling ideas.

It revealed itself in a much simpler way.

By looking.

Not outward, but inward – if that word can be used. Not inward as in turning attention to a place, but inward as in observing what is already happening, without adding anything to it.

There was a noticing.

Thoughts were appearing.
Sensations were appearing.
Perceptions were appearing.

And along with them, a subtle assumption persisted – that there was someone to whom all this was happening. Someone at the centre. Someone who was aware.

But when this "someone" was looked for directly, it was not found.

There were thoughts about a self.
There were images, memories, identities.
There was a voice that said "I".

But the one it referred to did not appear anywhere outside of those thoughts. The observer, it seemed, was also part of what was being observed. This did not come as a dramatic realisation.

There was no moment of achievement, no sense of "I have found it." If anything, it was the opposite.

Something that had always been assumed began to lose its solidity.

The centre was not there.
And yet, nothing was missing.
Experience continued.

Seeing continued.
Hearing continued.
Thinking continued.
Living continued.

But the sense that there was a separate entity controlling or owning all of this began to dissolve.

Actions happened, but there was no clear doer behind them.
Thoughts arose, but no thinker could be located.
Decisions appeared, but without a central decision–maker.

Life was unfolding, just as before. Only the assumption of "me" at the centre had weakened.

This is where the earlier questions take on a different meaning.

If there is no fixed "I" at the centre of experience, then what is it that is aware?

Not as a concept.
Not as a theory.
But as a fact of immediate experience.

There is awareness.

But it does not belong to anyone.
It does not carry a name.
It does not have a boundary.

It does not begin or end with the body in any directly observable way.

It is simply present.

In this seeing, the idea of a journey begins to fall apart.

If there is no separate "someone" to travel, what would it mean to arrive anywhere?

If what is being sought is already present, what is there to attain?

This is why so many masters pointed back, again and again, to the same simple enquiry:

Who am I?

Not to produce an answer. But to dissolve the questioner.

And when the questioner is not found, something unexpected remains.

Not emptiness in the sense of absence.
But emptiness as openness.

A clarity without centre.
A presence without identity.
A life that is happening, without being owned.

This is not the end of the enquiry.

If anything, it is the beginning of a different kind of understanding. One that does not move through accumulation, but through seeing.

And from here, the question is no longer:

"What is the truth?"

But:
"What remains, when what is not true is no longer held?"

At this point, it becomes helpful to pause and listen – not to new ideas, but to voices that have already walked this terrain and pointed, with remarkable clarity, to what cannot be grasped.

One such voice is that of Seng–ts'an, the Third Patriarch of Zen, whose verses in the Hsin Hsin Ming (Faith in Mind) carry a simplicity that cuts through centuries of thought.

He begins with a statement that, if taken seriously, unsettles the entire search:

"*The Great Way is not difficult for those who have no preferences.*"

At first glance, this seems almost too simple.

But what is preference here?

Not just liking or disliking, but the deeper movement of the mind that is constantly:

Choosing
Comparing
Seeking one state over another

This movement is the very structure of the "I".

To prefer is to sustain the one who prefers.

And so, the "difficulty" of the Way is not in its complexity, but in our inability to stop dividing experience.

"*When love and hate are both absent, everything becomes clear and undisguised.*"

This is not indifference.

It is the absence of psychological division.

When the mind is no longer projecting:
"this should be"
"this should not be"

then what remains is directness.
Reality is no longer filtered through resistance or grasping.

And in that, clarity is not created – it is revealed.

"*The slightest distinction, however, sets heaven and earth infinitely apart.*"

This is where the subtlety deepens.

The distinction here is not intellectual.

It is the almost invisible movement of separation:

observer and observed
self and other
seeker and truth

The moment this division appears, the simplicity of what is becomes fragmented.

And from that fragmentation, the entire structure of seeking begins.

"*To return to the root is to find the meaning, but to pursue appearances is to miss the source.*"

The "root" is not something hidden in a distant place.

It is what is already present before thought divides it.

But the mind is conditioned to move outward:
toward concepts
toward explanations
toward experiences

And in doing so, it misses what is already here.

Not because it is absent, but because it is too immediate to be noticed as an object.

"*When thought is in bondage, the truth is hidden; when thought is free, the truth appears.*"

This does not mean stopping thought by force.

It points to something more subtle.

Thought is in bondage when it is believed.

When it defines reality.
When it creates the "I" and is taken to be true.
When that grip loosens, thought may still arise – but it no longer obscures.

It becomes just another movement within awareness.

"*The wise do not strive; the foolish bind themselves.*"

Here again, the teaching turns everything upside down.

The search itself becomes the barrier.

Because striving assumes:
something is missing
someone must attain it

But if no such "someone" exists in the way it is assumed, then striving only reinforces the illusion.

"*In this world of Suchness, there is neither self nor other.*"

This is perhaps the clearest statement.

Not as a philosophy, but as a direct seeing.

The division we take for granted – between "me" and "world" – is not found when looked at closely.

There is experience.
There is awareness.
But the boundary is conceptual.

And without that boundary, what remains is what Zen calls *Suchness* – things as they are, without separation.

These verses do not offer a path in the conventional sense.

They do not describe a process of becoming.

They point, again and again, to what is already the case – obscured only by the movement of thought and the assumption of a separate self.

And perhaps this is why they feel both simple and elusive.

Because they do not give the mind something to do.

They reveal that there may be nothing to do.

In another stream of human enquiry, far removed from philosophical argument or scientific explanation, a different kind of dialogue unfolds.

It is said to take place between Shiva and Parvati.

Parvati asks a question that echoes through all seekers:

What is the nature of reality?
What is this universe?
What is the essence behind all appearances?
How may it be known directly?

This is not a request for belief.

It is a demand for direct knowing.

Shiva does not respond with a doctrine. He can if he wants to. But doesn't.
He does not offer a system to be followed over time.
He does not ask for faith.

Instead, what unfolds is something remarkable.

A series of methods.

Not rituals.
Not philosophies.
But precise invitations to look.

The Vigyan Bhairav Tantra presents over a hundred such methods – 112 to be exact.

Each one begins exactly where you are.
Not in a monastery.
Not in withdrawal from life.
But in the immediacy of experience.

In breath.
In sensation.
In sound.
In the gap between two thoughts.
In the moment of surprise.
In the space between inhalation and exhalation.

One method says:

Be aware of the moment between two breaths.

Not the inhalation.
Not the exhalation.

But the subtle pause.

In that pause, there is no movement.
No direction.
No becoming.

Only presence.

Another points to sound:
Listen, not to the meaning of the sound, but to the pure hearing itself.

Before interpretation.
Before naming.

Just the raw fact of hearing.

In that, the listener and the sound begin to dissolve into a single field of experience.

Another suggests:

In a moment of intense emotion – fear, joy, anger – do not move away.

Enter it fully.

Without resistance.
Without story.
At the peak of intensity, something breaks open.

Not the emotion itself, but the one who claims it.

These methods are not techniques in the conventional sense.

They are not steps to achieve something in the future.

They are doorways.

Each one pointing to a simple but radical possibility: That what is being sought is already present but overlooked because attention is always moving.

What is striking is their subtlety.

They do not attempt to change reality.
They do not attempt to improve the individual.
They do not aim at becoming anything.
They simply reveal.

And in this, they align with what has been seen earlier.

If there is no fixed "I" at the centre, then who is there to transform?

If awareness is already present, then what needs to be attained?

Here, a quiet distinction begins to emerge.

Spirituality, in its essence, does not ask for belief. It asks for seeing. It asks for a direct encounter with what is already the case.

Not tomorrow.
Not after discipline.
Not through accumulation.

But now.

Religion, on the other hand, often begins with truth – but turns it into structure.

It offers explanations.
It provides narratives.
It gives form to the formless.
And in doing so, it serves a role.

It shapes behaviour.
It creates ethical frameworks.
It prepares the ground.

But it can also become something else.
A system of belief.

To believe is to accept something as true without seeing it directly.

Even if the belief is profound, beautiful, or sacred, it remains second–hand.

It may guide action.
It may refine conduct.
It may create the conditions for enquiry.

But it does not, by itself, dissolve the illusion of the self.

Because the "I" can believe.

The "I" can adopt spirituality.
The "I" can become more refined, more disciplined, more knowledgeable.

And yet, remain intact.

The methods of the Vigyan Bhairav Tantra cut through this.

They do not allow the "I" to stand at a distance.
They do not ask you to become something.

They bring you face to face with experience – so directly that the one who seeks begins to fade.

And perhaps this is the essential difference.

Belief adds something to the mind.
Seeing removes what was never there.
In that removal, nothing new is gained.

And yet, everything is different.

And so, after all the enquiry, all the questions, all the attempts to understand…

something very simple remains.

Life is happening.

Breath is moving.
Sounds are appearing.
Thoughts are arising and dissolving.
The body is functioning.
The world is unfolding.

All of it, just as it always has.

Nothing has been added.

No new object has been found.
No hidden entity has been discovered.
No final answer has been secured.

If anything, something has fallen away.

The assumption of a centre.
The idea of a separate "I" who stands behind experience.
The quiet belief that there is someone who must arrive somewhere.

And in the absence of that…

there is a different kind of simplicity.

Not created.
Not achieved.
Not owned.

Just present.

The mind may still ask:

What is this?
Is this consciousness?
Is this the truth?

But these questions no longer carry the same urgency.

They arise, like everything else, and pass.

What remains does not need a name.

It cannot be held as knowledge.
It cannot be organised into a system.
It cannot be claimed as an experience.
Because there is no one at the centre to claim it.

And yet, nothing is missing.

Perhaps this is what the sages pointed to in their own ways.

Not a destination.
Not a reward.
Not an attainment.

But the end of a certain kind of confusion.

The search, which once felt necessary, begins to lose its ground. Not because something has been found. But because the one who was searching is no longer solid.

From here, life continues.

Ordinary.
Unremarkable.
And yet, quietly complete.

There may still be questions about consciousness, about continuity, about what unfolds beyond the limits of a single lifetime.

But these questions no longer arise from fear, or from the need to secure a self. They arise, if at all, from curiosity within the unfolding of life itself.

And perhaps that is enough.

Not an answer.
Not a conclusion.
Not a belief.

Just this.

What we call consciousness, what appears as awareness, what animates this living system may not belong to an individual at all.

The brain may function as a conductor,
a remarkable instrument through which experience is organised,
through which life expresses itself in coherent form.

But what it conducts is not owned.

It does not begin with the body, nor does it end in the way we imagine.
Like a wave rising in the ocean,
forming briefly as a distinct movement,
and then dissolving back–

what we call a lifetime may be a temporary configuration within a much larger continuity.

In this light, even the idea of rebirth shifts.

Not as a "person" continuing, not as a soul travelling from one place to another, but as a continuity of pattern, a movement of cause and effect, a subtle transmission within the fabric of existence itself.

What traditions call karma need not belong to an individual self.

It may simply be the unfolding of conditions, carried forward, expressed again, until understanding dissolves, the very basis of that movement.

And when that is seen–

not as an idea, but as a fact in direct experience – then something comes to rest.

Not because everything has been explained. But because the need to explain begins to fade.

From here, nothing needs to be added.

And nothing needs to be removed.

There is nothing to interpret here.
No meaning to extract.
No conclusion to arrive at.
No path from here to somewhere else.

Because there is no one that travels.
And there is no destination to reach.
In this quiet, even the ancient questions fall away.

A monk once asked by disciple Hui–Chung to Zen Master Hui–Neng:

"I have left my home to become a monk, and my aspiration is to attain Buddhahood. How should I use my mind?"

The answer came:
"Buddhahood is attained when there is no mind which is to be used for the task."

The monk persisted:

"When there is no mind to be used for the task, who can ever attain Buddhahood?"

And the reply:

"By no–mind the task is accomplished by itself. Buddha, too, has no mind."

This is not a teaching to be understood.

It does not offer instruction.

It simply removes the ground beneath the question.
If there is no mind to use,
no self to refine,
no one to attain–

then what remains?

Not an answer.
Not an experience.
Not even a realisation that can be held.

Just this.

Without interpretation.
Without movement.
Without becoming.

And in this, the search finds no place to continue.

Not because it has reached its end,
but because it was never needed.

(silence).

For Further Reading

The books listed here are those that speak most directly to the themes explored in these pages – physics, perception, consciousness, and the nature of the self. They are not cited as authorities but offered as companions for anyone who wishes to go further.

On Physics, Time, and the Nature of Reality

Carlo Rovelli – The Order of Time (2018). A lyrical and rigorous exploration of why time feels like it flows, what physics actually says about its structure, and what remains when our intuitions about past and future are dismantled.

Carlo Rovelli – Helgoland (2021). An elegant account of relational quantum mechanics – the view that quantum states are not absolute but defined only in relation to observers – and its implications for how we understand reality.

Richard Feynman – QED: The Strange Theory of Light and Matter (1985). Feynman's own account of quantum electrodynamics – how light and matter interact at the deepest level – written for the general reader with characteristic clarity and wit.

Sean Carroll – Something Deeply Hidden (2019). A clear–eyed defence of the many–worlds interpretation of quantum mechanics, and an accessible account of why the measurement problem remains one of the deepest unsolved questions in physics.

Roger Penrose – The Emperor's New Mind (1989). Penrose's landmark argument that human consciousness cannot be fully explained by computation, drawing on Gödel's incompleteness theorems, quantum mechanics, and the physics of spacetime.

On Consciousness and Perception

Anil Seth – Being You: A New Science of Consciousness (2021). The neuroscientist who coined the phrase "controlled hallucination" explains how the brain constructs our experience of reality and selfhood – and why that construction is not the same as illusion.

David Chalmers – The Conscious Mind (1996). The philosophical work that introduced the "hard problem" of consciousness into wide discussion – why physical brain processes should give rise to subjective experience at all – and argued that no purely materialist explanation can fully account for it.

Bernardo Kastrup – Why Materialism Is Baloney (2014). A rigorous philosophical case for analytic idealism – the view that consciousness is fundamental and matter is its expression – drawing on both Western philosophy and the insights of contemplative traditions.

On the Self, No–Self, and Contemplative Enquiry

Ramana Maharshi – Who Am I? (1902, trans. various). The foundational text of Ramana's teaching – a direct, spare enquiry into the nature of the "I" and what remains when the seeker is sought.

Nisargadatta Maharaj – I Am That (1973, trans. Maurice Frydman). Conversations recorded in Mumbai in the early 1970s that repeatedly press toward the same recognition: awareness is not a possession of the person but the ground within which the person appears.

Rupert Spira – Being Aware of Being Aware (2017). A short, precise meditation on the nature of pure awareness – what remains when attention turns back on itself rather than forward toward objects, thoughts, or experiences.

J. Krishnamurti – The First and Last Freedom (1954). Krishnamurti's clearest statement of his central insight: that psychological time – the movement of thought between past and future – is the source of the self's suffering, and that freedom is not achieved through accumulation but through direct seeing.

Sam Harris – Waking Up: A Guide to Spirituality Without Religion (2014). A neuroscientist's case that the insights of contemplative traditions – particularly the dissolution of the sense of self – are genuinely available through secular practice and worth pursuing without any framework of belief.

Vigyan Bhairav Tantra – attributed to Shiva, (trans. Various). A classical tantric text presented as a dialogue between Shiva and Devi, offering 112 contemplative methods that use breath, sensation, perception, silence, and shock as gateways beyond the ordinary mind and the sense of a separate self. There is a narrative version by Osho.

Sengcan – Hsin Hsin Ming (c. 600 CE, trans. various). One of the earliest and most beloved Chan texts – a spare, poetic expression of non–duality that points beyond preference, division, and conceptual grasping toward the effortless clarity of the undivided mind. There is a narrative version by Osho.

D. T. Suzuki – The Zen Doctrine of No–Mind (1949). A lucid introduction to the Zen understanding of mushin (wu–nein), or "no–mind" – not the absence of awareness, but freedom from fixation, self–consciousness, and the dividing activity of thought.

On Buddhism and the Philosophy of Mind

Thich Nhat Hanh – The Heart of the Buddha's Teaching (1998). A clear and accessible guide to the core teachings of the Buddha – impermanence, interbeing, dependent origination, and the nature of suffering – written for readers with no prior background in Buddhist thought.

Francisco Varela, Evan Thompson & Eleanor Rosch – The Embodied Mind (1991). A foundational work in cognitive science that puts Buddhist philosophy and phenomenology into direct dialogue – arguing that mind and world co–arise through embodied experience rather than being separately given.

Nagarjuna – Mulamadhyamakakarika (trans. various). The foundational text of Madhyamaka philosophy – a radical deconstruction of essence, identity, causation, and selfhood through the doctrine of emptiness and dependent origination.

Walpola Rahula – What the Buddha Taught (1959). Still one of the clearest introductions to early Buddhist teaching – especially on anatta, impermanence, suffering, and the practical path of insight.

Douglas R. Hofstadter & Daniel C. Dennett (eds.) – The Mind's I (1981). A provocative collection of essays and thought experiments on consciousness, identity, self–reference, and the illusion of a unified self, drawing together philosophy, cognitive science, AI, and literature.

On Vedanta, Advaita, and Indian Philosophy

Swami Vivekananda – Jnana Yoga (1899). The path of knowledge as Vivekananda understood it – an enquiry into the nature of the self that begins not with belief or ritual but with the question of what, precisely, we are.

Sri Nisargadatta Maharaj – Prior to Consciousness (1985, ed. Jean Dunn). Late dialogues that press even further than I Am That – pointing toward what remains prior even to the sense of awareness itself.

Shankara – Vivekachudamani (trans. various). A classic Advaita Vedanta text on discrimination between the real and the transient, the nature of Atman and Brahman, and the dissolution of false identification with body and mind.

Ashtavakra Gita – (Author unknown, composed c. 1st–14th century CE, trans. Various). One of the most direct non–dual texts in the Indian tradition – uncompromising in its insistence that the Self is ever free, untouched, and beyond all becoming.

Where Science and Contemplation Meet

David Bohm – Wholeness and the Implicate Order (1980). A physicist's argument that the universe is a single unbroken whole – the "implicate order" – of which visible reality is only the "explicate" surface. One of the few scientific texts that reaches toward something resembling the Vedantic vision of non–separation.

Fritjof Capra – The Tao of Physics (1975). An early and influential exploration of the parallels between modern physics – relativity, quantum mechanics, field theory – and the worldviews of Eastern mystical traditions. Best read as a source of resonances, not as a proof of identity.

Alan Watts – The Way of Zen (1957). Still the most readable introduction to Zen thought for Western readers – tracing the movement from Chinese and Indian origins through the Japanese tradition, with particular attention to the experience of sudden insight and what lies beyond the grasping mind.

Evan Thompson – Waking, Dreaming, Being (2015). A sophisticated dialogue between neuroscience, philosophy of mind, phenomenology, and Indian contemplative traditions, examining waking consciousness, dreaming, selfhood, and the limits of reductive materialism.

Erwin Schrodinger – Mind and Matter (1958). A short but influential meditation by one of quantum theory's founders on the relation between consciousness and the physical world, including reflections that resonate strongly with Vedantic thought.

ABOUT THE AUTHOR

Vivek Sharma is based in Melbourne, Australia, where he works in education and consulting. Alongside his professional life, a longstanding curiosity about the nature of reality and human experience gradually deepened into something more deliberate.

That curiosity led first to reading across philosophical and spiritual traditions in early years, and later to direct practice under a teacher several decades ago. Since then, the enquiry has continued in a quieter, more observational form – less about seeking answers, and more about examining what is assumed

www.ingramcontent.com/pod-product-compliance
Lightning Source LLC
LaVergne TN
LVHW091128080826
845145LV00008B/2084